Praise for *Wh*

"A writer that has experienced the promises about which she writes is of tremendous value in a day of messages laced with preservatives. The life and words in the book, "When the Son Speaks a Promise" are organic, fresh, and wholesome nutrition to those struggling to believe the promises of God."
-Rev. Kim Moore, MSW, LCCT, LPC

"In this book, Felecia shares her relentless journey of faith to wholeness and offers every reader the HOPE that God's healing power is available to us all in our time of need and in our day to day walk with Him."
-Rebecca Keener, President –Heritage Christian Fellowship, Inc. Host – Always More TV

"We have known Felecia for more than 25 years. The trials and sufferings she has experienced in life have proven to strengthen her faith and made her an overcomer in this life. This book will bring encouragement and revelation when facing difficulties as you look to the Son, Jesus Christ, the Author and finisher of your faith."
-Apostle Michael and Michelle Leavell, Joy Christian Center

"Felecia Doyle has gone through an experience that will restore a passion for the promises of God. In this book, she presents truth in a simple but profound way. The more you read this book the more you will rely on and trust the promises of God. We all face storms of life, but we have an anchor, the promises of God, which holds us steady until the storm ceases. In 71 years of ministry I have learned that pain and suffering are a gift from God to draw us closer to Him."

-Dr. Hugh Skelton, Missions Support Services, Inc.

"Where does life find you today? What difficult times are you enduring? Well, you can be encouraged because the powerful promises of God leave no phase or issue of life uncovered! Felecia Doyle, my friend and a mighty woman of God, has experienced near death tragedy - turned miracle that has given her a platform for ministry. Her book will no doubt be an encouragement to many. Her collections of scriptures, faith, hope and confidence in God during recovery are all powerful. You will be blessed by the book "When the Son Speaks a Promise" written by one of God's great women."

-Pastor Katie Franklin – Wisdom Club Ministry, Convalescent Home Ministry, Comfort Carrier Ministry

When the Son Speaks a Promise

Copyright © 2018 by Felecia Doyle
ISBN -13: 978-1722161453

Cover design by Jill Haack

Italics in Scripture quotations are the author's emphasis.
Unless otherwise indicated, Scripture quotations are from:
The Holy Bible: King James Version (KJV)
Other Scripture quotations are from:
The Holy Bible: New King James Version® (NKJV)
© 1982 by Thomas Nelson, Inc.
Used by permission. All rights reserved.
The Holy Bible, New International Version ® *(NIV)*
© 1973, 1978, 1984, 2011 by Biblica, Inc.®
Used by permission. All rights reserved worldwide.

ALL RIGHTS RESERVED
No part of this publication may be reproduced, stored in a retrieval system, or transmitted, in any form or by any means—electronic, mechanical, photocopying, recording or otherwise—without prior written permission.

Printed in the United States of America

Acknowledgments
THIS BOOK IS FOR THOSE WHO ASK THE QUESTION WHAT DOES IT MEAN TO BELIEVE ON HIS PROMISES?

Thanks to God for giving me the courage to share my testimony and opportunity to write my first book. I've heard the saying, "everyone has a book within them." I'm thankful for God's promise to never leave me or forsake me, and to know that I can trust Him with my life. I'm grateful that He healed me physically and spiritually.

Another great blessing in my life is my beautiful family. Dad and Mom committed their hearts to give and serve others. I'm thankful for their modeling the Christian walk of prayer, reading the Word and worshipping God. They are pillars of God's grace and they depend on the Lord with all their hearts. It was not a perfect family, we had our issues like most, but we always turned to God in the good and bad times. Mom taught me to lean on the promises of God's Word through every situation I faced. Thank you for my brothers, Greg and James, who have played an integral part in who I am today. I can think of no greater family than mine to have been honored with by God. Praise the Lord for my husband, George who is the love of my life. You have been a constant support throughout our marriage. I love you with all my heart. No matter what we face, I'm thankful I can count on you to always be by my side.

Thanks, too, to my children and grandchildren, Shauntara, Chelsea, Patrick, Axel, and Trinity. I'm thankful that my children and grandchildren love the Lord with all their heart. I wrote this book to leave a legacy of truth and words of encouragement to believe in the promises of God. And to also encourage my family to do whatever God has destined them to do while they are living on this earth.

Message from Shauntara - My mother lives to share God's love and her testimony with the world. Love you Mom and glad God kept you under His wing that day!

Message from Chelsea – My mother recovered fully and is a walking testimony to God's favor. My mom is strong and beautiful in every way. I learned that God looks at your response. God wants us to praise Him for the good times, and He wants us to worship Him through the storm. God is looking for your faith to soar through the storm. God will never leave you or forsake you. Through this incident, He confirmed to me His lasting promises.

Message from Phyllis Pizzino – I was in total shock when I heard my friend was in an accident. I asked myself, "How could this happen to such a good person that everyone needs so much?" I went home and spent the night on my knees praying to God to save my friend. I had not done that since my son's stroke. Terrible events force us to seek God, but we shouldn't wait till something like this happens to turn to God. That was the biggest lesson I learned from my friend's accident. I also realized my selfishness, because I needed her here. Felecia's kindness and positive outlook were so important to me.

Message from Rebecca Keener - My husband and I were among those who sat with Felecia's family in the Surgical Waiting Room during one of her surgeries and prayed. Many of her friends, students and co-workers stood with Felecia and her family over the long months of her recovery. We believed God would miraculously heal and raise her up and He did!

Special thanks to my friend, Diane O'Connell, who has been a mentor to me for several years. She has an excellent gift for the body of Christ. We met at a prayer meeting, and God purposed our hearts together from that time forward. Thank you for modeling the faithfulness of God, His love, wisdom, and truth. I pray God continues to use you for His kingdom. Thank you for your prayers during the most challenging time of my life.

Thanks, to my friend, Karol Scarborough, who filled my teaching position at Flowery Branch High School for four months while I was recovering from my accident. I appreciate you and your gift of excellence. Thank you for editing my book and helping me to fulfill my dream.

Thanks to my colleagues and beautiful friends who supported me and prayed me through to the other side of my healing. I hope this book encourages you to trust God and lean on his promises no matter what problem you're facing. God bless you all.

Special thanks for the hospital visits, prayers, and meals provided by Free Chapel ministry. Thanks to Atlanta Medical Center and the Emergency personnel who were strategically guided by God to airlift me to the hospital. Every procedure performed, and every service rendered was for God's glory towards my physical healing.

Last but not least, thanks to all my wonderful readers who've bought my book and spread the word to their friends. Thank you for your support, and may God bless you all. I pray God will speak a promise over your life every day.

When the Son Speaks a Promise

Acknowledgements 1
Introduction 7

My First Trial - September 27, 2011 12
My Second Trial - May 27, 2014 24

Seven Principles that Allow Your Trial to 27
    1-Give You a Thankful Heart 29
    2-Transform You into His Image 32
    3-Test your Faith in the Lord 36
    4-Silence the Enemy by Your Testimony 39
    5-Connect the Promises of God and Prayer 44
    6-Be Covered by Grace, Mercy & Love 49
    7-Complete what God has started in You 55
Personal Confessions 59
Healing Scriptures 63
Conclusion 66

Spoken Promises 69
When the Son Speaks a Promise About Your
Christian Path
    Walking in God's Perfect Will 70
    Walking in the Word 72
    Walking in Love 73
    Walking in Humility 74
    Walking in Praise 75
    Walking in Prayer 76
    Walking in Trust 78
    Walking in Faith/Confidence 80
    Walking in Patience 82
    Walking in Hope 84
    Walking in Peace 86

Focus on the Promise and not the Problem

When the Son Speaks a Promise for the Needs of Others
    Deliverance from Satan 88
    Employment 90
    Peace in a Troubled Marriage 91
    Overcoming Rejection in Marriage 92
    Husbands/Wives 93
    Child's Future 94
    Rebellious Teenager 95

When the Son Speaks a Promise Concerning Personal Concerns
    Living Free from Worry 97
    Victory Over Fear 99
    Renewing Your Mind 101
    When Troubles Hit Your Life 102
    Living Free from Depression 103
    Walking in Freedom 105
    Living Free from Guilt 107
    Living Free from Loneliness 108
    Living Free from a Negative Self-Concept 109
    Living Free from Rejection 111
    Walking in Forgiveness 113

When the Son Speaks a Promise about Caring for Others
    Comforting Others 114
    Encouraging Others 115
    Praying for Safety and Protection 116
    Praying for Someone Who Has Lost a Loved One .. 118
    Salvation 119

When the Son Speaks a Promise about People
and Nations
    Nations and Continents 121
    Schools Systems 122
    Members of the Armed Forces 123
    Missionaries 125
    Peace of Jerusalem 126

Focus on the Promise and not the Problem

Introduction

Have you ever asked this question, 'Why me?' or 'Why am I going through this?' No one escapes problems or challenges in life, but there is good news -- Jesus (Son) promises that we can overcome if we live in Him. Jesus tells us in John 16:33 that we will have tribulation, trials, distress, and frustration in this world, but in spite of that, we can be of good cheer and take heart. Why? Because He has overcome the world, and when we live in Him, we become an overcomer, too!

> *"Beloved, do not think it strange concerning the fiery trial which is to try you, as though some strange thing happened to you; but rejoice to the extent that you partake of Christ's sufferings, that when His glory is revealed, you may also be glad with exceeding joy. Yet, if anyone suffers as a Christian, let him not be ashamed, but let him glorify God in this matter. Therefore, let those who suffer according to the will of God commit their souls to Him in doing good, as to a faithful Creator."* 1 Peter 4:12-13, 16, 19 NKJV

First Peter 4:12 tells you not to think it strange concerning the trial you are facing but rejoice and be glad with exceeding joy if you partake of Christ's suffering. You may ask yourself how can you glorify God and allow your trial to enhance your joy. Do you find yourself worried by the crashing waves of turmoil in your life, or are you experiencing "*the peace of God, which surpasses all understanding*" Philippians 4:7 NKJV? Unless you have faith to believe in the promises of God, anytime a problem or challenge comes into your life, the enemy plays with your thoughts, and you begin to live in fear and despair. Second Timothy 1:7 NKJV tells us that God has not given us a spirit of fear, but of power and love and a sound mind. Do not allow the enemy to steal your joy, peace and rest. The enemy will bring thoughts of the worst possible outcome in your mind, and his whole purpose is to keep you from experiencing God's will in your life and distract you from the truth of God's Word. "*The thief comes only to steal and kill and destroy; I have come that they may have life, and have it to the full.*" *John 10:10 NIV*

God wants you to live an abundant life with Him on a daily basis, not just when everything is going smoothly. He will always, always take care of everything that concerns you. No matter how hard it gets in life and no matter what you are facing, you are an overcomer. Jesus has promised He will never leave you nor forsake you. Deuteronomy 31:6b NIV The trial or tribulation you are facing may be a recent separation or divorce, troubled marriage, a health-related issue, a car wreck, loss of a job, business failure, personal injury or illness, major illness or death of a spouse or close family member, stress, rebellious son or daughter, drug or alcohol addiction the list goes on and on. Trials and tribulations can come out of nowhere, and the question resurfaces in your mind, "Why me?" You may be asking yourself, "Can I honestly rejoice and be glad with exceeding joy no matter what I'm facing?" Only through the grace and mercy of God can you praise Him in, for and through your problems. Allow your trial to be a source of pleasure because any trial you face strengthens your faith in God. When you are in the midst of the tribulation or trial, what you are experiencing may be painful, hurtful, grieving and seems like it will never go away. After you read these encouraging words, I want you to remember He suffered for you because He loved you before you were ever born. *"Indeed, the very hairs of your head are all numbered."* Luke 12:7a NIV *"For God so loved the world, that he gave his only begotten Son, that whoever believeth in him should not perish, but have everlasting life."* John 3:16 KJV

This trial may have you holding on with the tips of your fingernails. When I was facing my trials, I would imagine how I could move forward each day. Jesus died for all my pain, all my suffering, and all my discomfort. I whispered this prayer every day, 'Jesus (Son) if I can see the next morning sun, I know I can make another day while you strengthen me'. Not in my strength but by His strength He makes me whole. Just like you count on the sun rising every day, you can count on the Son (Jesus) to speak promises about how powerful He is to take care of you through any trial or circumstance. *"But he said to me, 'My grace is sufficient for you, for my power is made perfect in weakness.' Therefore, I will boast all the more gladly about my weaknesses, so that Christ's power may rest on me."* 2 Corinthians. 12:9 NIV

It's by Christ's power and strength that you will overcome, wake up and start another day. In this book, I want to share what Jesus has shown me through His promises as I walk daily in this Christian life. As believers, we sometimes want to believe that we are facing difficulty because we deserve it, or we did something wrong or the devil did it. I don't want to focus on the problem, the difficulty or the devil. I want to focus on what His Word promises every believer, so we can live victoriously through Him. Through these trials, God showed me seven amazing principles about Himself and His greatness. In the pages that follow, I want to share with you how God used the greatest trials in my life to bring great miracles.

Focus on the Promise and not the Problem

My First Trial

It seemed like any other fall day. The air was cool and crisp, and I was looking forward to a great afternoon with my friend, Diane. On September 27, 2011, I was taking Diane horseback riding at Lanier Islands for her birthday. I'm not a rider but I wanted to give her a birthday she would always remember. As we began to get ready for the trail ride (with very little instruction), I noticed my horse was being very stubborn and not listening to the handler. After about 10 minutes on the trail, my horse was not following the guide. When the guide's horse went left, my horse would go right throughout the entire trail. I asked the guide, "Why is my horse going in the opposite direction from where you are leading, and she said that he wants to lead." I thought it was very strange, but I assumed she knew what was going on. Fifteen minutes later, my horse saw where he could get ahead of the guide and he took off frantically forward as fast as he could. My only reaction was to pull back on the reigns and close my eyes. When the horse threw me, there was a terrifying moment of silence; I thought the world had stopped and my mind was spinning, trying to figure out what to do next. In desperation, I tried to focus and comprehend what was happening. My thoughts were scrambled, going in and out, disjointed from reasoning. Diane sat opposite of me keeping me calm while I began to gather my thoughts. In my mind, I asked myself, "Is this it, am I dying like this?" I landed tremendously hard on the left side of my body. I knew I had fallen really hard on the ground. I was feeling stunned, sore and awkward, but I seemed to be alright. I could see Diane and I was answering the questions she was asking me. I was somewhat disoriented, and Diane was telling the guide to go get help right now. The guide had to run back to the stable and call the emergency personnel. Diane told me later that she didn't want to startle me, but she was very scared that she was losing her friend. She knew from my responses that I was in deep danger. How could a moment change my life forever? Time seemed to stand still, blood was dripping from the left side of my head and my body felt really sore. I'm thankful for the helmet. It saved my life from serious brain injury. I fractured my cheekbone and had to get several stitches to repair the cut near my eye. The white of my left eye remained red for several days. My body felt as heavy as a tree trunk. I was not able to move too quickly. I had scrapes on my hands and knees and my watch flew off my arm where I landed. I was utterly defenseless and feeling like I had done something wrong. Why was this happening to me? I had no idea why the horse ran off and wasn't sure where it had gone. My only focus was to determine the extent of my injuries and get the help I needed.

The paramedics could not bring the ambulance to me because the trail was too deep in the woods. Diane began to pray and ask God to intervene; she saw death slowly approaching. I had to be carried out on a stretcher to the helicopter. I am thankful that the medical team decided to airlift me from there to the trauma hospital. As I was in the helicopter traveling to Atlanta Medical Center (AMC), I felt such a wave of peace come over me, and I knew angels were covering me. I still didn't know what was injured, but it had to be extremely bad for them to airlift me away to a trauma hospital. I was thinking about how I was going to survive this helicopter ride, because I get very nauseous when I fly. I was praying that I would not get sick while they were transporting me to AMC.

Diane couldn't ride with me due to the limited capacity of the helicopter, so she got in touch with my family to meet me at the hospital. My husband, George was home preparing to go to work that evening, and he never answers the home phone. When Diane called George, she said "Hi George, this is Diane. Felecia has been seriously injured in an accident during our horseback riding outing at Lanier Islands. She is being airlifted to the Atlanta Medical Center. I am talking to the pilots now and she is stable." George remembers, "Before I could get my questions out, Diane said she would have to go with the EMT team, and she would see me later at the hospital. Wow, this simple two-minute phone call started a chain of life events that have led to the writing of this book. I am so thankful for God's presence in my life. His grace and mercy seem more tangible in times of tragedy and pain. From the moment I learned of the accident, and throughout the subsequent days of treatment and recovery, I felt God's hands on my shoulders. When I experienced fear of a negative outcome, I prayed, and God's answered to calmed my fears."

My oldest daughter, Shauntara was at work when she received the call about my accident. She thought it was me calling, but it was her dad telling her that I had been in a severe accident and was currently at the hospital in surgery. She asked her dad if I was alive and at the time her dad was unsure about my condition. Shauntara immediately grabbed her keys and purse and ran out of the building in tears. She prayed the entire way home and texted everyone she knew to start praying. When she got home, she was finally able to sit and cry. At the time, my grandkids were still pretty young and did not know why their mom was crying. Tara told them that "Mimi (what they call me) has been in an accident and mommy is very sad because I don't know if Mimi is going to make it or not." My granddaughter, Trinity, was five at the time, and she took my daughter's hand very calmly and said, "well mommy we need to pray." Tara looked at my granddaughter in shock and immediately stopped crying. She said, "God used a child to help me do what I should have been doing all along. PRAY! So, everyone in the room (Christopher, Axel, Trinity, CJ, Beebop and myself) all held hands and prayed at the leading of a 5-year-old child." Even though my daughter has been a Christian pretty much her whole life, she had never experienced this type of peace and love during what was a very emotional time, and she knew at that moment her trust needed to be in God, not her fear. The Psalm of David, Chapter 23 is what sustained her and what she proclaimed over me during the 10 hours of not knowing whether I was alive or not.

> *"The Lord is my shepherd; I shall not want. He maketh me to lie down in green pastures: he leadeth me beside the still waters. He restoreth my soul: he leadeth me in the paths of righteousness for his name's sake. Yea, though I walk through the valley of the shadow of death, I will fear no evil: for thou art with me; thy rod and thy staff they comfort me. Thou preparest a table*

> *before me in the presence of mine enemies: thou anointest my head with oil; my cup runneth over. Surely goodness and mercy shall follow me all the days of my life: and I will dwell in the house of the Lord forever."* Psalm 23 KJV

Later that night, Tara was up praying for my healing and that God would spare my life. My daughter lives in California. About 12am their time (which would have been 3am my time), she felt a sense of peace from God that everything was going to be okay and she was finally able to fall asleep. When my daughter arrived at the hospital, she was speaking to Diane and sharing her prayer experience and how God had given her an overwhelming sense of peace. Diane shared that around midnight the night of the accident, she had been praying and suddenly felt a release from God that I was going to live. My husband, George, was listening to this conversation and said, "you know that was about the time that the surgeon who was operating on your mom was able to stop the bleeding, and she began to respond to the second blood transfusion. She is not out of the woods yet, but at least she is not bleeding anymore." At that very moment, they all had felt the peace of God at the very same time, even though they were in different states. God is good, and He hears our prayers.

When my daughter, Chelsea heard the news, she had already left work at Challenged Child for the day and had stopped at the gas station. As she waited for her tank to fill, she received a phone call from her dad. He started off with, "There has been an accident with mom." She said, "I remember it taking a few seconds to process his words initially. I then started asking a lot of questions, 'Where is she? Was it a car accident? What happened?' I knew he could tell I was about to break down while I spouted out question after question. Daddy was so calm while he was explaining everything so that I would not break down over the phone. He told me to come home right away, we would ride to the hospital together and he would discuss the details then. As I drove to the house, I could only think the worse. I still couldn't wrap my head around the fact that my mother was injured in any way. After I got home, my dad was waiting in the driveway, and we left immediately."

"On the way to the hospital, I finally realized the accident was with a horse. As we drove, we discussed what we knew about the accident. Talking about it helped me conceptualize what had really happened. We did not know the extent of her injuries or the severity of the situation at the time. I distinctly remember that my dad never overreacted or freaked out during this whole time. He was calm and reassuring as we drove. His response to this situation enabled me to remain calm as well. Looking back, I know that God was in that car and His presence was clear. There was no other way to describe the sense of peace we both felt in that car ride. After arriving at the hospital, we were told my mom was in surgery. I looked at my dad, I couldn't imagine what was going through his head at that moment. This was his wife in surgery and neither one of us knew exactly what was happening in the operating room. When we were finally able to speak with the doctor and heard the severity of my mom's injuries, it shook me to the core. All of the strength I was trying to display for my dad vanished. All of the reassurance I had had on the ride up completely left my body. I was broken. A sense of fear swarmed over my body and I began to cry uncontrollably. I knew I had to remove myself from where my family had gathered. As I sat alone, all I could think about was my mom in pain. I thought about the injuries that she had sustained from the accident. I thought about the doctors who were painstakingly operating on her in the other room. All of these thoughts left me feeling helpless and anxious. I knew I could not get through this on my own strength or through my own power. I knew I had to put my trust in God's Word and His promises. In my weakness, my God is strong. I knew the only way I was going to get through this was to keep reciting scriptures in my head over and over. I declared, "Do not fear, for I am with you; do not be discouraged, for I am your God. I will strengthen you and help you; I will uphold you with my righteous right hand." I kept saying, "I love you, Lord, my strength. The Lord is my rock, my stronghold and my deliverer in whom I take refuge, my shield and the horn of my salvation, my stronghold." I prayed these promises over myself, my mom, and the doctors. After a while, the feelings of helplessness and anxiety diminished, and a wave of peace and comfort filled my body. I knew my mom would get through this. I knew that my faith would also strengthen because of this experience as well."

When my son, Patrick, received the news, he was very calm and collected. His friends were wondering why he wasn't upset. He wasn't concerned or surprised about my accident. He believes that everything is purposed, thus the outcome is determined before the event. Even the notion of calling the incident an "accident" is incorrect because our Father in Heaven does not make mistakes and is perfect in every way. Patrick knew in his heart that I would be ok.

After arriving at Atlanta Medical Center, I was taken immediately for exploratory laparotomy (abdominal wall surgery) and nephrectomy (surgical removal of a kidney). I had internal bleeding from what appeared to be an adrenal vessel which needed to be ligated (tied together). I suffered multiple left-side rib fractures as well as bruising along the left side of the abdomen, and I had a ruptured spleen. The splenic laceration was substantial which led to my spleen being removed. I was hemorrhaging from the left renal vein which was repaired. I was given two ten packs of blood due to the tremendous blood loss. Dr. Spence was my surgeon, and his team did a tremendous job saving my life. The doctors could not determine what the outcome would be until I woke up.

My family waited in the waiting room for hours. Thankfully, they received periodic updates from the operating surgeon. Every time they received an update, it was moving in the right direction. I was in the operating room for roughly six hours. The surgeons were great. God's hands were on every one of them.

I was in ICU for three days with a ventilator and several tubes coming out of my body. I woke up the next day, and I was giving orders about what should be completed at school.

I was concerned about my students, but one thing I learned through all of this is that life continues on with or without you. God gave me a scripture to help me with this trial, 2 Timothy 1:7 KJV *"For God hath not given us the spirit of fear; but of power, and of love, and of a sound mind."* My faith was being challenged. I've been a Christian for a long time, but the challenge was can I truly trust God and rely on His promises in my darkest hour. I relied only on His promises to heal, deliver and set me free from this injury and pain. I believed I would be restored to better health even with these injuries. I was in the hospital for seven days, hoping each day to go home, but I was having this constant pain on my left side, and my blood pressure would not stabilize. I began spiking a fever, and a CT scan of the chest and abdomen showed an ischemic (insufficient blood supply) left kidney. Dr. Spence determined that I had developed necrosis (it had died) of my left kidney and it had to be removed. I was in tears because I never thought I would have to face another surgery with all the tremendous pain I had already endured. The night before the surgery, I told my husband and Diane that if I didn't make it through this second surgery, I'm at peace to go home with Jesus. I didn't want them to be worried or scared about the outcome. The Word declares in Psalm 118:17 KJV that, *"I shall not die, but live, and declare the works of the Lord."* My mom, family and friends spent the night with me at the hospital while I was recovering from my accident. I was in the hospital for 21 days, and it took 4½ months of physical therapy before I was able to return to work and resume normal activities. My right kidney is functioning extremely well, and my blood pressure is normal.

God spared my life and gave me a second chance to share about His goodness and grace. He's a good Father and I love Him with all of my heart. The enemy tried to kill me, but God had a better, more excellent, plan. He told me that I will live and declare the works of the Lord. The works of the Lord for me is serving the hurting and those who need to know about God's love. It was a beautiful, fall day when this happened, and God turned my darkest hours into preparation for my best days. I am so thankful for all the prayers and God's grace over my life. I am thankful for my family, church family, friends and acquaintances for their prayers and complete support during this difficult time.

My Second Trial

Over the years, I've had friends and students suffer with severe migraines. Not having ever been a migraine sufferer, I greatly empathized but could not sympathize with people who suffer with this pain on a daily basis. Then it happened to me. Words cannot describe the mind-numbing pain that started on May 20, 2014. It felt like a dagger piercing through the front of my forehead. I tried Tylenol, Goody's Powder and over the counter migraine medicine. I went to the doctor on May 23 to see if I could get some relief from this constant headache pain. I don't have headaches, so it was very strange for me to be experiencing this type of pain. The doctor gave me some migraine medicine but could not determine why I was experiencing this pain. That following weekend, as the pain continued, I was extremely sick with nausea and vomiting, barely able to get out of bed. Chelsea drove me to school on Tuesday, May 27 to turn in some paperwork because I was too weak to drive. After attending the faculty meeting, I was planning to return home and go back to sleep because the pain had subsided a little. On the way to my car, two of my colleagues who are nurses, Kathy and Rose, encouraged me to go to the emergency room. I left school and went to the emergency room at Northeast Georgia Medical Center to determine what was causing my headache. If you have ever been to the emergency room, you know there's always a wait, but with my visit, God's hand was strategically guiding the medical staff. I was taken immediately to triage and I filled out the necessary paperwork to be admitted to a room. After discussing the symptoms with the emergency room doctor, he ordered an ultrasound. After the ultrasound, the emergency room doctor approached me, looking like he had seen a ghost. He asked me what had I done, had I been in an accident, had I fallen or had anyone hit me in the head? He said I had a subdural hematoma (SDH), which is a type of traumatic brain injury. With a SDH, blood gathers between the inner layer of the dura mater (tough fibrous membrane that envelops the brain and spinal cord), putting pressure on the brain and causing damage to brain tissue. Subdural hematomas are often life-threatening. The doctor was astonished and amazed that I had not had any trauma to cause this type of injury. I had to have emergency brain surgery to remove the blood from the left side of my brain. I was in ICU for three days to drain the blood from underneath my skull. I spent one night in a regular room and then I was able to go home. I have recovered completely with no limitations or any neurological damage, and I greatly appreciate the thoughts and prayers from my church, family and friends. I am thankful for God's perfect timing and exceptional grace over my life AGAIN. God performed a second miracle that saved my life, and I give Him all the glory and honor.

God is in control over every trial and tribulation we face. God spared my life for a second time and I know he has great plans and purpose for me. I'm in His divine hands and I'm allowing Him to lead me in His direct path. I want to encourage you to use God's promises to answer the 'Why me?' or 'Why am I going through this?' question you may be asking. When the Son speaks a promise, you can count on Him to stand with you and to see you through every challenge or difficulty. In the following pages, I want to share seven amazing principles God showed me in His Word that gave me sustained determination, and continue to strengthen and encourage me on my journey.

Seven Principles that Allow Your Trial To...

Remembering what God has brought me through is pivotal in my faith journey. When those hard situations arise – and they do arise – I can think back on all that God has led me out of, how He has healed me, restored me and redeemed me. It is important for believers to remember that God knows the whole story of our lives. Sometimes He shelters us from things, while other times He sustains us in them and brings us through to the other side. If we allow Him to, God will lead us along our journey. I use journaling as a way to meditate on the promises of God and reflect on what He taught me through scripture reading, praying and worshipping in my quiet time. One of the great joys of Bible journaling is seeing evidences of God's grace, goodness, and faithfulness throughout my life. I encourage you to use journaling to strengthen your walk with the Lord. Write down the nuggets of wisdom from the Word and your prayer time that the Holy Spirit reveals in your spirit. When trials and temptations come, you may find that the words from your journaling are just what you need to stand strong in God's strength against the attack of the enemy. Through journaling, I get to see how His hand has gradually led me, month by month, year by year, and how He has held me by

His grace. I've outlined seven principles for you to journalize your thoughts and prayers for you to recite. Whether you choose to journal or not, you can trust that God rewards those who diligently seek Him.

Principle 1

... Give you a Thankful Heart

"In everything give thanks: for this is the will of God in Christ Jesus concerning you." 1 Thessalonians 5:18 KJV

Two weeks before my horseback riding accident I was praising God and thanking Him for all He had done in my life. I felt a spirit of thankfulness flood my soul. It was an overwhelming flood of His love and Him assuring me that He is with me. I began to just thank Him for everything. Looking back, I believe God was preparing me to trust Him and be confident that He would see me through anything I face. No matter what you face, God says to give thanks in everything for this is His will for you. I thank Him for allowing me to survive this accident, I thank Him for my health, strength and being able to see another day. Give thanks to Him for His mercy, grace, goodness, and faithfulness over your life. Give thanks for the air you breath, the food you eat and every provision. With every circumstance you face, be blessed by thanking and praising God.

Journal Experience:

Write down what you are thankful for.

_____
_____
_____
_____
_____
_____
_____
_____
_____

How can you turn your circumstance into a blessing of thankfulness?

_____
_____
_____
_____
_____
_____
_____
_____
_____
_____
_____

Thanksgiving Prayer:

Heavenly Father, I give thanks to You today, because You are a good, good Father. Your faithful love continues forever. Everything in heaven, everything on earth; the kingdom is all yours! You've raised Yourself high over all and I trust You to take care of me when I face any trial. You hold strength and power in the palm of Your hand to build up and strengthen all. And here I am, O God, giving thanks to You, praising Your splendid Name. I thank You for Your unfailing love, righteousness and marvelous works; I will dance and sing praises to the name of the Lord Most High. I will enter His gates with thanksgiving and enter His courtyards with praise! Thank You, for waking me up this morning; thank You for giving me life, breath and strength. Bless Your Holy name! Hallelujah! I give thanks to Adonai; for He is good, for His mercy, grace and steadfast love endures forever. Praise the Lord!

Principle 2

...Transform You into His Image

It's not enough to tell someone to pray, read their Bible or go to church when they're in pain, brokenhearted, disappointed and feel like giving up. I was hospitalized for 21 days; my strength was gone. There were days I didn't have the energy to pray or read my Bible. But I knew without a shadow of a doubt who I am in Christ. Christ in me is my hope, my strength, my fortress and my redeemer. I relied on the promises of God's Word to move me pass this feeling of helplessness. God is the potter, and I am the clay. He wants to mold and transform me into His image. The shaping, molding and transformation process can be painful. I believe a certain amount of conflict is what God will use to make us more like Him. Trials and tribulations will either make you or break you in your spiritual walk with the Lord. The conflict will show you what you are made of and who you trust. Severe adversity will cause you to persevere to your miracle, or it will cause you to give up on God and what He wants to do with your life.

"So, do not fear, for I am with you; do not be dismayed, for I am your God. I will strengthen you and help you; I will uphold you with my

righteous right hand. Isaiah 41:10 NKJV *"The LORD himself goes before you and will be with you; he will never leave you nor forsake you. Do not be afraid; do not be discouraged."* Deuteronomy 31:8 NIV *"For I know the plans I have for you," declares the Lord, "plans to prosper you and not to harm you, plans to give you hope and a future."* Jeremiah 29:11 NIV

God knows the plans He has for us. In Jeremiah 29:11, He promises to give us prosperity, hope and a future. But as we live this journey called life, let's be reminded that maturity comes through persevering through trials, not escaping them. As we learn to persevere, we find joy. In the midst of suffering, we can rely on Jeremiah 29:11 that God will take away our suffering and give us hope instead.

Journal Experience:

Write four promises from the three scriptures listed above.
_____
_____
_____
_____
_____
_____
_____
_____
_____
_____
_____
_____
_____
_____
_____
_____
_____
_____
_____
_____
_____
_____
_____
_____
_____
_____
_____

Prayer of Hope

Heavenly Father, You said to be confident because Jesus is our hope. Though the enemy comes against us on every side, we can hope in the Lord. I'm thankful that You will never forget the afflicted and those in need. I'm thankful that You, God, are a refuge for the oppressed, a stronghold in times of trouble. Those who know Your name trust in You, Lord, because You have never forsaken those who seek you. Those who put their hope in You will never be put to shame. Our souls can find rest in God our Father, because You are good to those whose seek You and rely totally on You. Hope is like a golden cord connecting us to heaven. This cord helps us to hold our head up high, no matter what we're facing. Thank you for transforming us into your image. We know that You will never leave our side, and You will never let go of our hand. My soul finds rest in You, God, because my hope comes from You. Your Word promises to give us prosperity, hope and a future. Thank You for Your continued hope, in Jesus' name.

Principle 3

...Test your Faith in the Lord

The reason God will allow a certain amount of trials and tribulations to come in your life is to test your faith levels in Him. When everything is going at its best, it's easy to have a high level of faith. But when conflict approaches, many Christians will lose their faith in God.

Smith Wigglesworth, a great apostle of faith, had a very catchy saying. He always said, "from great fights will come great faith." In other words, you cannot develop great faith in the Lord unless you first have your faith tested. God will allow trials and tribulations to come your way to see if you will trust Him and keep your faith in His promises no matter how dark and hopeless things may look in the natural.

Assuming that this trial would pass, and I would not continue to suffer, was my hope. Can you believe that, even through trials, you will one day see the glory of God fulfilled in your life and the lives of others? It's a choice to believe or not to believe in the promises of God no matter what comes your way. Hebrews 11:1 KJV reminds us that *"Now faith is the substance of things hoped for, the evidence of things not seen."* Webster describes "substance" as a thing or physical matter or material from which something is made. Faith for me was tangible because I hoped to be physically and spiritually restored from my accident. The evidence of my faith took four months, but I chose to believe the promise given in Hebrews 11:1. I give God all the glory and honor for His goodness and grace towards me. I would never have made it without God by my side, strengthening me daily to do a little more than I did the day before. *"For all the promises of God in him are yea, and in him Amen, unto the glory of God by us."* 2 Corinthians 1:20 KJV

Journal Experience:

Is God testing your faith, what does faith mean to you?

_____
_____
_____
_____
_____
_____
_____

What are you believing God to do in your life?

_____
_____
_____
_____
_____
_____

Prayer of Believing by Faith

Father, I believe that faith is the substance of things hoped for and the evidence of things not seen. Today, I trust You to help me see beyond my physical realm of circumstances into the spiritual realm through my faith. I call those things that be not as though they are. Your Word teaches that whoever hears what Jesus says, and believes in the One who sent Him has eternal life. Jesus, You are the way, the truth and the life. No one comes to the Father except through you. He that believeth on Jesus, as the scripture has said, out of his belly shall flow rivers of living water. Lord, I believe. I have faith that I have already received whatever I've prayed for, and it will be mine. I am standing firm in my faith, acting courageously, being strong. May the Word of God be like a belt around my waist and may God's justice protect me like armor. I am a winner because the battle has already been won through the Lord!

Principle 4

...Silence the Enemy by the Word of Your Testimony

In Revelation 12:11a, John says that we overcome by the word of our testimony and the blood of the Lamb. I'm thankful that Jesus paid the price for my sins. I was raised in a Christian home and went to church every time the doors were opened, but I did not have a relationship with Jesus. I lived a hypocritical life through my teen years and young adult life. But one night, 38 years ago, I was gloriously saved and touch by the hand of the Lord. It was a night I will never forget. My mom invited me to a small Pentecostal church in Martin, Georgia. I don't remember what the pastor was preaching, but when he asked the congregation to come to the altar to receive Christ, I surrendered. It was like experiencing the book of Acts. I heard and felt a rushing wind surround me and I gave everything to Jesus. From that night, I was changed, and my heart was in His hands. I began a new walk with the Lord and yielded to His promises to save me, deliver me and set me free.

The Christian walk is a process, and over the years, I have had to daily lay down my flesh and walk in the Spirit. The Holy Spirit is, and has been, my comfort and peace, and He continues to teach me how to live victoriously as a Christian. My eyes were open to the truth of God's love and grace. After receiving the baptism of the Holy Spirit, my Christian walk was empowered by another dimension of God's grace. In Acts 1:5 NKJV Jesus promised, *"For John truly baptized with water, but you shall be baptized with the Holy Spirit not many days from now."* Then in verse 8 He says, *"But you shall receive power, after that the Holy Spirit is come upon you; and you shall be witnesses to me in Jerusalem, and in all Judaea, and Samaria, and to the end of the earth"* The fulfillment of these two promises came on the day of Pentecost.

> *"And suddenly there came a sound from heaven as of a rushing mighty wind, and it filled all the house where they were sitting. And there appeared unto them cloven tongues like as of fire, and it sat upon each of them. And they were all filled with the Holy Ghost, and began to speak in other tongues, as the Spirit gave them utterance."*
> Acts 2:2–4 KJV

It doesn't matter what you have done; His arms are open to receive you today. He died for your sins so that you would have eternal life. If you do not know Jesus as your Savior and

Lord, don't delay, get it settled in your heart so that you can experience life more abundantly. Make Him Lord of your life today, renounce your past life with Satan and close the door to any of his devices. It's not complicated, pray the following prayer in faith: Lord Jesus, I ask you to come into my heart and be Lord of my life according to Romans 10:9-10 KJV. *"That if thou shalt confess with thy mouth the Lord Jesus, and shall believe in thine heart that God has raised him from the dead, thou shall be saved. For with the heart man believeth unto righteousness, and with the mouth confession is made unto salvation."* I do that now. I confess that Jesus is Lord, and I believe in my heart that God raised Jesus from the dead. Thank you for forgiving me of all my sins and saving me today, in Jesus' name.

According to Ephesians 2:8 NIV *"For it is by grace you have been saved, through faith—and this is not from yourselves, it is the gift of God."* Jesus has paid it all. He took the keys of death and hell. He came to overcome the world and release every captive that is held by the enemy. The storm will not last always, and trials are an opportunity for a testimony. God gets the glory when we go through a hard time and stand strong, trusting in the Lord until He delivers. Be free by sharing your testimony and silencing the enemy.

Journal Experience:

Write your testimony.

_____
_____
_____
_____
_____
_____
_____
_____
_____
_____
_____
_____
_____
_____
_____
_____
_____
_____
_____
_____
_____
_____
_____
_____
_____
_____
_____

Focus on the Promise and not the Problem

Prayer to Receive the Infilling of the Holy Spirit

If you made that confession, you are a new creation in Christ, old things have passed away, and now all things become new in Jesus' name. Now that you are reborn and a child of Almighty God, you can pray to receive the infilling of the Holy Spirit. Pray: Heavenly Father, I am your child, for I believe in my heart that Jesus has been raised from the dead, and I have confessed Him as Lord. *"If ye then, being evil, know how to give good gifts unto your children: how much more shall your heavenly Father give the Holy Spirit to them that ask him?"* Luke 11:13. KJV I'm asking you to fill me now with the Holy Spirit. I step into the fullness and power that I desire in the name of Jesus. I confess that I am a Spirit-filled Christian. I fully expect to speak in tongues as the Spirit gives me utterance in the name of Jesus. Praise the Lord!

Principle 5

...Make the Connection Between the Promises of God and Prayer

The promises of God should inspire us to pray. A few years after my encounter with God, I had the opportunity to be a part of a remarkable women's organization called Aglow International. I'm thankful for that season of my life because I was mentored by some prayer warriors who knew how to touch God through their prayers. We would do prayer rides in Gainesville, and I listened and learned how to pray. Over the years, God showed me that by mediating on His Word, and speaking the Word back to Him in prayer, I'm speaking His promises over my life, especially during times of trials.

> *"So is my word that goes out from my mouth: it will not return to me empty, but will accomplish what I desire and achieve the purpose for which I sent it."* Isaiah 55:11. NIV

Praying is exciting because we are talking to God. The Word commands us to pray and it makes promises to us of what God will do if we pray. James 5:16 NIV says to "...*confess your sins to each other and pray for each other so that you may be healed."* In Hebrews 4:12 KJV it states, *"The word of God is quick, and powerful, and sharper than any two-edged sword, piercing even to the dividing asunder of soul and spirit, and of the joints and marrow, is a discerner of the thoughts and intents of the heart."* In Proverbs 30:5 KJV it states, *"Every word of God is pure, he is a shield unto them that put their trust in him."*

As a believer, you can be confident that God's Word will cut to the core of any circumstance you face and will discern the intent and motives of your heart. Use the promises of God to change the atmosphere of your situation. The prayer of a righteous person is powerful and effective. I have included several healing scriptures in the next part of this book that I use when I need healing for myself or I am praying for others to be healed. The promises of God inspire me to pray so I can see the fulfillment of God's will over my life and the lives of others. Jesus taught His disciples that they *"ought always to pray and not lose heart"*. Luke 18:1 NKJV Don't give in, don't give up and don't lose heart when tribulation comes. Trust that Jesus will make a way for you. Paul commands in 1 Thessalonians 5:17 KJV to *"Pray without ceasing."* Paul is referring to an attitude of surrender that you can have all the time. When you allow your thoughts to focus on worry, fear, disappointment, discouragement and anger, what are these thoughts doing for your situation? Nothing but getting in the way of you fulfilling the promises of God. It's a distraction the enemy uses to get your thoughts off the promises of God and leaning on feelings of worry and unbelief. Quickly turn every thought into prayer and every prayer into Thanksgiving. *"Do not be anxious about anything, but in every situation, by prayer and petition, with thanksgiving, present your requests to God."* Philippians 4:6 NIV

Paul taught the believers at Colossae in Colossians 4:2 NIV to devote themselves to prayer and to be watchful and thankful and he encouraged the Ephesian believers in Ephesians 6:18 to see prayer as a weapon to use in fighting spiritual battles. As we go through our day, prayer should be our first response to every anxious thought, fearful situation and every task we pursue. A lack of prayer causes us to depend on ourselves instead of depending on God who has all power and authority.

Prayer must be the foundation of every Christian walk. The promises of God are our weapons against the enemy. When Satan tempted Jesus, Jesus used the Word of God to put him in his place. In Matthew 4:4 NIV, Jesus said, *"It is written: 'Man shall not live on bread alone, but on every word, that comes from the mouth of God."* Proverbs 4:20-23 admonishes us to attend to God's Word and keep it in the midst of our heart because it is life to those who look for it and health to all flesh. As believers, the Word of God has to be a part of us like the skin on our body. We are to be clothed with the Word. God is our portion, and every Word that comes out of the mouth of God reveals Him and His power, majesty and love. Today, make the connection between the promises of God and prayer, and allow it to be a cornerstone in your spiritual life.

Journal Experience:

Are you anxious, fearful, worried or discouraged? Write your thoughts to God and allow His promises to speak to you as you reflect on the verses referenced above.

_____
_____
_____
_____
_____
_____
_____
_____
_____
_____
_____
_____
_____
_____
_____
_____

Recite the Lord's Prayer

Every waking moment is to be lived in an awareness that God is with us and engaged in our thoughts and actions. In Mark 1:35, Jesus got up early in the morning, while it was still dark, went off to a solitary place where he prayed.

Luke 11:1 NIV says, *"One day Jesus was praying in a certain place. When he finished, one of his disciples spoke to him. "Lord," he said, "teach us to pray, just as John taught his disciples."* Matthew 6:9-15 NIV *This, then, is how you should pray: 'Our Father in heaven, hallowed be your name, your kingdom come, your will be done, on earth as it is in heaven. Give us today our daily bread. And forgive us our debts, as we also have forgiven our debtors. And lead us not into temptation, but deliver us from the evil one. For if you forgive other people when they sin against you, your heavenly Father will also forgive you. But if you do not forgive others their sins, your Father will not forgive your sins.'"*

Principle 6

…Be Covered by God's Grace, Mercy & Love

> *"But none of these things move me, neither count I my life dear unto myself, so that I might finish my course with joy, and the ministry, which I have received of the Lord Jesus, to testify the gospel of the grace of God."* Acts 20:24

I believe God allows you to suffer in order to testify and show the grace, goodness and love of God. I ask myself where I would be without God's grace over my life. He has protected me from danger I didn't even know was there. I am only worthy through Him and what Jesus has done in my life; it's all based on the grace that I do not deserve. *"Let us then approach God's throne of grace with confidence, so that we may receive mercy and find grace to help us in our time of need."* Hebrews 4:16 NIV I am in desperate need of God's grace and mercy, and I found Him in my time of need. That's another awesome promise that He speaks to those that believe in Him. You can approach God's throne of grace with confidence anytime you face a need. God is attracted to impossible situations. Matthew 19:26 NIV says *"Jesus looked at them and said, 'With man this is impossible, but with God all things are possible.'"* When you cry out with a loud voice, my God will answer you because He loves you that much! The following scripture encourages you to approach God with confidence so that you will receive mercy and find grace in your time of need. *"Grace, mercy, and peace from God the Father and from Jesus Christ, the Father's Son, will be with us in truth and love."* 2 John 1:3 NIV

Do you know without any doubt that, no matter what you have done, God loves you unconditionally? His love is eternal and everlasting. God showed His love by sending His Son (Jesus) into the world so that you can be saved. Ephesians 2:4-5 KJV says "*But God, who is rich in mercy, for his great love wherewith he loved us, even when we were dead in sins, hath quickened us together with Christ, by grace are ye saved.*" God's love is not like the love communicated by many in today's culture: a love that's conditional and convenient. God's love never changes, and nothing can separate you from the love of God. Romans 8:38-39 NIV speaks a promise from God about his love for you. *"For I am convinced that neither death nor life, neither angels nor demons, neither the present nor the future, nor any powers, neither height nor depth, or anything else in all creation, will be able to separate us from the love of God that is in Christ Jesus our Lord."* Trials will happen that will make you feel insecure and separated from the love of God. God promises that NOTHING can ever separate you from His love. Death, life, angels, demons, fear for today, worries about tomorrow, not even powers of hell, no power in the sky above or in the earth below, nothing in all creation will EVER be able to separate you from the love of God. Wow! Can you shout hallelujah for this promise!!! Circumstances will never be so bad that you will be separated from the love of God. He will never break this promise concerning His love for you.

> *"God so loved the world that he gave his only begotten son that whoever believes in Him shall never die but have eternal life."* John 3:16 NIV
> *"Dear friends, let us love one another, for love comes from God. Everyone who loves has been born of God and knows God. Whoever does not love does not know God, because God is love. This is how God showed his love among us: He sent his one and only Son into the world that we might live through him."* I John 4:7-9 NIV"

And so we know and rely on the love God has for us. God is love. Whoever lives in love lives in God, and God in them." 1 John 4:16 NIV

Love closes the gap between doubt and unbelief as you trust in His love and allow God to live in you.

Journal Experience:

Write down your experiences of God's grace and mercy in your life.

_____
_____
_____
_____
_____
_____
_____
_____
_____
_____

What does Romans 8:38-39 speak to your heart about God's love?

_____
_____
_____
_____
_____
_____
_____
_____
_____
_____
_____
_____
_____
_____

Focus on the Promise and not the Problem

Prayer of the Love of God

Heavenly Father, for most of my life I have tried to earn Your love and gain Your approval. It seems the more I try to get You to love me the more I find that I fail You. Today, I realize that I can't earn Your love because You love me unconditionally. I also know that You sent Your Son Jesus into this world so that I would have eternal life. All who live in love, live in God, and God lives in them. Thank You for showing me in Romans 8:38-39 that nothing can separate me from Your love, Your grace or Your mercy. Thank You that your approval does not rely on me at all, but rests on the promise that if I believe in the Lord Jesus as my Savior, I am accepted by You. Thank You for showing me that Your love for me is not dependent on what I say or what I do but rests on what Jesus did on the cross for me. I am a new creation in Christ, clothed in His righteousness. Thank You for Your unconditional and everlasting love in the precious name of Jesus.

Principle 7

...Complete what God has Started in you

God planned your destiny long before you were ever born. He prepared your life from the foundation of the earth. Psalm 139:16 NIV says, *"...all the days ordained for me were written in your book before one of them came to be."* You were born into this world with a God-given purpose and destiny. Jesus said, *"Before I formed you in the womb I knew you, before you were born I set you apart; I appointed you as my prophet to the nations."* Jeremiah 1:5 NIV You were set apart and appointed to do God's divine will. Your plan may not be apparent but be confident that God has a divine purpose for you to complete.

> *"Being confident of this very thing, that He which hath begun a good work in you will perform it until the day of Jesus Christ."* Philippians 1:6 KJV *"For we are God's handiwork, created in Christ Jesus to do good works, which God prepared in advance for us to do."* Ephesians 2:10 NIV

You have a choice on whether or not to say yes to God's plan for your life. The first step is asking Jesus to come into your heart and saying yes to all that He has in store for you. Do not delay accepting Him today. Jesus is the answer to everything you've ever wondered, thought or imagined. Take time to look at all that He has done in your life and let your faith rest on His Word and His promises to you.

You can be confident that Jesus has begun a good work in you and will continue to perfect it until He returns. You may have had a few setbacks and disappointments, but each day God gives you another chance to allow your problem to move you closer to Him. How many days do you have left? No one knows, except God. Ask yourself this question, "What can I do with the rest of my life to fulfill my destiny and God's divine purpose?" Allow your latter days to be greater than your former days. You are living in the best days of your life. Make every day count and begin now to pursue your destiny. Search and ask God to reveal your God-given purpose and do it with all your heart, mind and soul. Live the destiny now before it's too late!!!

Journal Experience:

What are some of the unique talents and experiences God has given you? What gets in the way of you fulfilling God's destiny for your life?

_____
_____
_____
_____
_____
_____
_____
_____
_____
_____
_____
_____
_____
_____
_____
_____
_____
_____
_____
_____
_____
_____
_____
_____

Focus on the Promise and not the Problem

Prayer Concerning Your Purpose and Destiny

Heavenly Father, I desire Your purpose and destiny for my life. I'm thankful that I'm Your masterpiece, created anew through Christ Jesus. You knew me before I was born, and You have given me a unique mixture of gifts, passions, abilities, talents and experiences. There is no one like me in this entire universe. You have promised in Your Word that You have begun a good work in me and will continue to perfect it until the day You return to take me to heaven. Forgive me for doubting Your plan and wasting precious moments. Help me today to step into what You have in store for my life. Remove any stumbling blocks that get in the way of me fulfilling Your destiny for my life. Holy Spirit give me wisdom, discernment and spiritual insight to walk in the direction God has chosen for me. Even when I mess up, I'm thankful You will turn my trial into destiny. I'm thankful that You will help me to fulfill my destiny in Jesus' mighty name.

Personal Confessions

As believers, we are to speak the things that the Word of God declares as truth. When we speak or confess out loud the promises of God, in faith, we receive them. Proverbs 18:20-21 KJV says *"A man's belly shall be satisfied with the fruit of his mouth; and with the increase of his lips shall he be filled. Death and life are in the power of the tongue; and they that love it shall eat the fruit thereof."* Circumstances are subject to change, and one thing that can cause them to do so is the confession of God's Word over a particular situation. The Word of God tells us to confess or speak out about the things we are believing God will do in our lives and He will bring it to pass. Isaiah 55:11 says, *"So shall my word be that goeth forth out of my mouth: it shall not return unto me void, but it shall accomplish that which I please, and it shall prosper in the thing whereto I sent it."* God commands us to read the Word, speak the Word and hear the Word. Sometimes our circumstances necessitate that we do all three (read, speak and hear) so that His promises become embedded in our spirit that we might stand firm against the attack of the enemy. Personal confessions based on the Word of God, spoken daily with confident assurance, will build our faith and move mountains.

Focus on the Promise and not the Problem

Here are some of my daily confessions:

Jesus Christ is Lord over my spirit, soul, and my body Philippians 2:11

Jesus has been made unto me wisdom, righteousness, sanctification, and redemption. 1 Corinthians 1:30

I can do all things through Christ who strengthens me. Philippians 4:13).

The Lord is my Shepherd; I shall not want (Psalms 23:1), because My God supplies all my needs according to His riches in glory by Christ Jesus (Philippians 4:19).

I do not fret or have anxiety about anything. I do not have a care because I cast all my cares upon him and he cares for me. (Philippians 4:6; 1 Peter 5:6-7).

I am the body of Christ. I am redeemed from the curse (Galatians 3:13) because Jesus took our infirmities and bore our sickness in His Own body (Matthew 8:17).

By His stripes I am healed; therefore, I forbid any sickness or disease to operate in my body. Every organ, every tissue of my body functions in the perfection in which God created it to function (1 Peter 2:24).

I honor God and bring glory to Him in my body and spirit (1 Corinthians 6:20).

I have the mind of Christ and hold the thoughts, feelings, and purposes of His heart (1 Corinthians 2:16).

I am a believer and not a doubter. I hold fast to my confession of faith (Hebrews 4:14).

My faith comes by hearing and hearing by the Word of God (Romans 10:17).

And Jesus is the author and finisher of my faith (Hebrews 12:2).

The love of God has been shed abroad in my heart by the Holy Ghost and His love abides in me richly. I keep myself in the kingdom of light, in love, in the Word, and the wicked one toucheth me not (Romans 5:5; 1 John 4:16; 1 John 5:18).

I tread on serpents and scorpions and over all the power of the enemy (Luke 10:19)

I take the shield of my faith and quench all the fiery darts of the wicked (Ephesians 6:16). Greater is He that is in me than he that is in the world (1 John 4:4). I am delivered from this present evil world (Galatians 1:4).

I am seated together with Christ in Heavenly places (Ephesians 2:6).
For the law of the Spirit of life in Christ Jesus hath made me free from the law of sin and death (Romans 8:2).

I do not allow fear to rule over me. For God has given me a Spirit of power, of love and of a sound mind (2 Timothy 1:7).

The Lord is on my side; I will not fear: what can man do to me? (Psalms 118:6)

I hear the voice of the Good Shepherd. I hear my Father's voice, and the voice of a stranger I will not follow (John 10:27).

I roll my works upon the Lord. I commit and trust them wholly to Him. He will cause my thoughts to become agreeable to His will, and so shall my plans be established and succeed (Proverbs 16:3).

I am a world overcomer, because I am born of God. I represent my Father and Jesus well. I am a productive member of the Body of Christ (1 John 5:4,5).

I am His workmanship created in Christ Jesus to do good works, which God prepared in advance for me to do (Ephesians 2:10,11).

For God is working in me, giving me the desire to obey Him and the power to do what pleases Him (Philippians 2:13).

Healing Scriptures

God's Word speaks of miraculous healing through Jesus Christ and faith in God. When you are overwhelmed with health problems, the Word of God can be your source of divine strength. This collection of Old and New Testament scriptures on healing will provide encouragement, strength, and comfort as you focus on God's healing power. Recite these scriptures out loud to the Lord and believe that you are healed in Jesus' name.

Old Testament Scriptures

"He said, "If you listen carefully to the Lord your God and do what is right in his eyes, if you pay attention to his commands and keep all his decrees, I will not bring on you any of the diseases I brought on the Egyptians, for I am the Lord, who heals you." Exodus 15:26 NIV

"Worship the LORD your God, and his blessing will be on your food and water. I will take away sickness from among you," Exodus 23:25 NIV

"LORD my God, I called to you for help, and you healed me." Psalms 30:2 NIV

"Have mercy on me, LORD, for I am faint; heal me, LORD, for my bones are in agony." Psalms 6:2

Focus on the Promise and not the Problem

"The LORD sustains them on their sickbed and restores them from their bed of illness." Psalms 41:3 NIV

"If you say, "The LORD is my refuge," and you make the Most High your dwelling, no harm will overtake you, no disaster will come near your tent." Psalms 91:9-10 NIV

"Praise the Lord, my soul, and forget not all his benefits -- Who forgives all your sins and heals all your diseases," Psalms 103:2-3 NIV

"He sent His word and healed them, and delivered them from their destructions." Psalms 107:20 KJV

"He heals the brokenhearted and binds up their wounds." Psalms 147:3 NIV

"My son, attend to my words; incline thine ear unto my sayings. Let them not depart from thine eyes; keep them in the midst of thine heart. For they are life unto those that find them, and health to all their flesh." Proverbs 4:20-22 KJV

"A cheerful heart is good medicine, but a crushed spirit dries up the bones." Proverbs 17:22 NIV

"But he was pierced for our transgressions, he was crushed for our iniquities; the punishment that brought us peace was on him, and by his wounds we are healed." Isaiah 53:5 NIV

"Heal me, Lord, and I shall be healed; save me and I will be saved, for you are the one I praise." Jeremiah 17:14 NIV

"But I will restore you to health and health your wounds, declares the Lord," Jeremiah 30:17 NIV

Focus on the Promise and not the Problem

"Behold, I will bring it health and cure, and I will cure them, and will reveal unto them the abundance of peace and truth." Jeremiah 33:6 KJV

New Testament Scriptures

"And when he had called unto him his twelve disciples, he gave them power against unclean spirits, to cast them out, and to heal all manner of sickness and all manner of disease." Matthew 10:1 KJV

"How God anointed Jesus of Nazareth with the Holy Ghost and with power: who went about doing good and healing all who were oppressed of the devil; for God was with him." Acts 10:38 KJV

"Is anyone among you sick? Let them call the elders of the church to pray over him and anoint them with oil in the name of the Lord. And the prayer offered in faith will make the sick person well; the Lord will raise them up. If they have sinned, they will be forgiven." James 5:14-15 NIV

"'He himself bore our sins'" in his body on the cross, so that we might die to sins and live for righteousness; 'by his wounds you have been healed.'" 1 Peter 2:24 NIV

"Beloved, I wish above all things that thou mayest prosper and be in health, even as thy soul prospereth." 3 John 1:2 KJV

Focus on the Promise and not the Problem

Conclusion

I wrote this book to help others overcome tragedies by trusting in the promises of the Son of God. Have you asked yourself, "How do I respond when I'm faced with a crisis? Do I respond with fear, anxiety, despair or do I quickly respond with what the Word of God promises?" Life will bring disappointment, heartache and unbearable pain, but be confident that Jesus will never let you down. Just like you can count on the sun rising every day, you can count on the Son (Jesus) to speak a promise to heal, restore and deliver you from any problem you may face. When trials and tribulations come, we know that we are protected from conflict based on the promise in Psalm 121:7 KJV *"The Lord shall preserve thee from all evil: he shall preserve thy soul."* We need conflict to grow and mature as a believer and exercise our faith muscles. I believe God allows conflict to mold and transform us into His perfect image. As you learn to pray the promises of God, instead of the problems, you will see your circumstances begin to unravel and dissolve. Every day I am challenged to believe and trust God. When you go through a hard time and you face trials that make you question who you are, allow it to shift you to a place of depending on His promises. Jesus helps me every day to stand and endure because without Him I don't know how I can make it. I remind myself of Philippians 4:13 KJV that *"I can do all things through Christ which strengthens me."* In my weakest and darkest hour, the light of His promise has shone brighter and brighter to lighten my path to healing, restoration and deliverance. Jesus is the same yesterday, today and forever. He defeated the enemy on the cross and shed His blood for your redemption. God said He will always be there for you in your good times and hard times. Seek Him through continuous prayer, not just when you have bad days, but every day of your life. Meditate on His Word and believe in His promises. He has given you everything you need to be a victorious Christian. We are living in the most exciting times to see the glory of God revealed in the earth. Thank you, Lord for all the promises of your Word. May I never forget that on my best day I still need God as desperately as I do on my worst day. I am forever changed when the Son speaks promises over my life.

*When the Son Speaks a Promise
Challenging Christians to:
live as an overcomer,
walk victoriously as a believer,
grow spiritually mature in Christ,
believe and not doubt God's promises,
know that God's promises are the same
yesterday, today and forever.*

*When the Son Speaks a Promise
Challenging Nonbelievers to know:
that God sent His Son Jesus to die
on the cross for their sins,
the Holy Spirit will be their
constant companion,
to rely on God to fill the
emptiness with His Love.*

Spoken Promises

Fervent prayer and the Word of God is powerful. When we combine these two foundations with the Holy Spirit, we unleash God to move on our behalf. Prayer is a place of refuge and help in difficult times. The pressures and troubles of life have a way of bringing an awareness of our dependency on God. The Apostle John states that: *"Now this is the confidence that we have in Him, that if we ask anything according to His will, He hears us. And if we know that He hears us, whatever we ask, we know that we have the petitions that we have asked of Him."* 1 John 5:14-15 KJV Our prayers are always in line with the will of God when we pray according to His Word. When you are lonely, sad, confused or need direction, these scriptures will bring the comfort of the Holy Spirit. Will you allow the Word of God to speak promises about your Christian walk, the needs of others, deliverance from Satan and his demonic forces, personal concerns, caring for others, people and nations? The topics outlined in the following pages are a guide to faith-building prayers based on the Word of God, promises already spoken over our lives. My prayer is that these scriptures will shape your prayers according to the Word of God, bringing freedom and victory to your life and the lives of others.

Focus on the Promise and not the Problem

When the Son Speaks a Promise About Your Christian Path

Walking in God's Perfect Will –

Exodus 31:3 (KJV)
And I have filled him with the spirit of God, in wisdom, and in understanding, and in knowledge, and in all manner of workmanship,

Proverbs 1:23 (KJV)
Turn you at my reproof: behold, I will pour out my spirit unto you, I will make known my words unto you.

Proverbs 2:2 (KJV)
So that thou incline thine ear unto wisdom, and apply thine heart to understanding;

Proverbs 2:6 (KJV)
For the Lord giveth wisdom: out of his mouth cometh knowledge and understanding.

Proverbs 4:7 (KJV)
Wisdom is the principal thing; therefore get wisdom: and with all thy getting get understanding.

Matthew 12:50 (KJV)
For whosoever shall do the will of my Father which is in heaven, the same is my brother, and sister, and mother.

Walking in God's Perfect Will –

Romans 2:18 (KJV)
And knowest his will, and approvest the things that are more excellent, being instructed out of the law;

John 6:37-38 (KJV)
All that the Father giveth me shall come to me; and him that cometh to me I will in no wise cast out. For I came down from heaven, not to do mine own will, but the will of him that sent me.

Colossians 1:9 (KJV)
For this cause we also, since the day we heard it, do not cease to pray for you, and to desire that ye might be filled with the knowledge of his will in all wisdom and spiritual understanding;

Acts 22:14 (KJV)
And he said, The God of our fathers hath chosen thee, that thou shouldest know his will, and see that Just One, and shouldest hear the voice of his mouth.

James 1:5 (KJV)
If any of you lack wisdom, let him ask of God, that giveth to all men liberally, and upbraideth not; and it shall be given him.

2 Peter 3:9 (KJV)
The Lord is not slack concerning his promise, as some men count slackness; but is longsuffering to us-ward, not willing that any should perish, but that all should come to repentance.

Walking in the Word –

Joshua 1:8 (KJV)
This book of the law shall not depart out of thy mouth; but thou shalt meditate therein day and night, that thou mayest observe to do according to all that is written therein: for then thou shalt make thy way prosperous, and then thou shalt have good success.

Psalm 119:11 (KJV)
Thy word have I hid in mine heart, that I might not sin against thee.

Psalm 119:89 (KJV)
For ever, O Lord, thy word is settled in heaven.

Hebrews 4:12 (KJV)
For the word of God is quick, and powerful, and sharper than any twoedged sword, piercing even to the dividing asunder of soul and spirit, and of the joints and marrow, and is a discerner of the thoughts and intents of the heart.

Hebrews 11:3 (KJV)
Through faith we understand that the worlds were framed by the word of God, so that things which are seen were not made of things which do appear.

Colossians 3:16 (KJV)
Let the word of Christ dwell in you richly in all wisdom; teaching and admonishing one another in psalms and hymns and spiritual songs, singing with grace in your hearts to the Lord.

Walking in Love –

Romans 5:5 (KJV)
And hope maketh not ashamed; because the love of God is shed abroad in our hearts by the Holy Ghost which is given unto us.

1 John 4:18-19 (KJV)
There is no fear in love; but perfect love casteth out fear: because fear hath torment. He that feareth is not made perfect in love. We love him, because he first loved us.

Matthew 5:44 (KJV)
But I say unto you, Love your enemies, bless them that curse you, do good to them that hate you, and pray for them which despitefully use you, and persecute you;

John 13:34 (KJV)
A new commandment I give unto you, That ye love one another; as I have loved you, that ye also love one another.

Ephesians 3:17-19 (KJV)
That Christ may dwell in your hearts by faith; that ye, being rooted and grounded in love, May be able to comprehend with all saints what is the breadth, and length, and depth, and height; And to know the love of Christ, which passeth knowledge, that ye might be filled with all the fulness of God.

1 John 2:5 (KJV)
But whoso keepeth his word, in him verily is the love of God perfected: hereby know we that we are in him.

Walking in Humility –

Proverbs 3:7-8 (KJV)
Be not wise in thine own eyes: fear the Lord, and depart from evil. It shall be health to thy navel, and marrow to thy bones.

Proverbs 22:4 (KJV)
By humility and the fear of the Lord are riches, and honour, and life.

1 Peter 5:5-6 (KJV)
Likewise, ye younger, submit yourselves unto the elder. Yea, all of you be subject one to another, and be clothed with humility: for God resisteth the proud, and giveth grace to the humble. Humble yourselves therefore under the mighty hand of God, that he may exalt you in due time:

Colossians 3:12-14 (KJV)
Put on therefore, as the elect of God, holy and beloved, bowels of mercies, kindness, humbleness of mind, meekness, longsuffering; Forbearing one another, and forgiving one another, if any man have a quarrel against any: even as Christ forgave you, so also do ye. And above all these things put on charity, which is the bond of perfectness.

James 4:10 (KJV)
Humble yourselves in the sight of the Lord, and he shall lift you up.

Focus on the Promise and not the Problem

Walking in Praise –

Judges 5:3 (KJV)
Hear, O ye kings; give ear, O ye princes; I, even I, will sing unto the Lord; I will sing praise to the Lord God of Israel.

Psalm 7:17 (KJV)
I will praise the Lord according to his righteousness: and will sing praise to the name of the Lord most high.

Psalm 71:8 (KJV)
Let my mouth be filled with thy praise and with thy honour all the day.

Psalm 92:1-2 (KJV)
It is a good thing to give thanks unto the Lord, and to sing praises unto thy name, O Most High: To shew forth thy lovingkindness in the morning, and thy faithfulness every night,

Hebrews 13:15 (KJV)
By him therefore let us offer the sacrifice of praise to God continually, that is, the fruit of our lips giving thanks to his name.

2 Samuel 22:4 (KJV)
I will call on the Lord, who is worthy to be praised: so shall I be saved from mine enemies.

2 Samuel 22:50 (KJV)
Therefore I will give thanks unto thee, O Lord, among the heathen, and I will sing praises unto thy name.

Focus on the Promise and not the Problem

Walking in Prayer –

2 Chronicles 7:12-14 (KJV)
And the Lord appeared to Solomon by night, and said unto him, I have heard thy prayer, and have chosen this place to myself for an house of sacrifice. If I shut up heaven that there be no rain, or if I command the locusts to devour the land, or if I send pestilence among my people. If my people, which are called by my name, shall humble themselves, and pray, and seek my face, and turn from their wicked ways; then will I hear from heaven, and will forgive their sin, and will heal their land.

Psalm 109:4 (KJV)
For my love they are my adversaries: but I give myself unto prayer.

Isaiah 55:11 (KJV)
So shall my word be that goeth forth out of my mouth: it shall not return unto me void, but it shall accomplish that which I please, and it shall prosper in the thing whereto I sent it.

Matthew 6:9-15 (KJV)
After this manner therefore pray ye: Our Father which art in heaven, Hallowed be thy name. Thy kingdom come, Thy will be done in earth, as it is in heaven. Give us this day our daily bread. And forgive us our debts, as we forgive our debtors. And lead us not into temptation, but deliver us from evil: For thine is the kingdom, and the power, and the glory, for ever. Amen. For if ye forgive men their trespasses, your heavenly Father will also forgive you: But if ye forgive not men their trespasses, neither will your Father forgive your trespasses.

Focus on the Promise and not the Problem

Walking in Prayer –

Luke 18:1 (KJV)
And he spake a parable unto them to this end, that men ought always to pray, and not to faint;

Romans 8:26-28 (KJV)
Likewise the Spirit also helpeth our infirmities: for we know not what we should pray for as we ought: but the Spirit itself maketh intercession for us with groanings which cannot be uttered. And he that searcheth the hearts knoweth what is the mind of the Spirit, because he maketh intercession for the saints according to the will of God. And we know that all things work together for good to them that love God, to them who are the called according to his purpose.

Philippians 4:6 King James Version (KJV)
Be careful for nothing; but in everything by prayer and supplication with thanksgiving let your requests be made known unto God.

Colossians 4:2 King James Version (KJV)
Continue in prayer, and watch in the same with thanksgiving;

1 Thessalonians 5:17 King James Version (KJV)
Pray without ceasing.

James 5:16 King James Version (KJV)
Confess your faults one to another, and pray one for another, that ye may be healed. The effectual fervent prayer of a righteous man availeth much.

1 John 1:9 King James Version (KJV)
If we confess our sins, he is faithful and just to forgive us our sins, and to cleanse us from all unrighteousness.

Walking in Trust –

Psalm 32:10-11 (KJV)
Many sorrows shall be to the wicked: but he that trusteth in the Lord, mercy shall compass him about. Be glad in the Lord, and rejoice, ye righteous: and shout for joy, all ye that are upright in heart.

Psalm 112:7 (KJV)
He shall not be afraid of evil tidings: his heart is fixed, trusting in the Lord.

Jeremiah 17:7-8 (KJV)
Blessed is the man that trusteth in the Lord, and whose hope the Lord is. For he shall be as a tree planted by the waters, and that spreadeth out her roots by the river, and shall not see when heat cometh, but her leaf shall be green; and shall not be careful in the year of drought, neither shall cease from yielding fruit.

1 Timothy 5:5 (KJV)
Now she that is a widow indeed, and desolate, trusteth in God, and continueth in supplications and prayers night and day.

Proverbs 3:5-6 (KJV)
Trust in the Lord with all thine heart; and lean not unto thine own understanding. In all thy ways acknowledge him, and he shall direct thy paths.

2 Samuel 22:31 (KJV)
As for God, his way is perfect; the word of the Lord is tried: he is a buckler to all them that trust in him.

Focus on the Promise and not the Problem

Walking in Trust –

Psalm 7:1 (KJV)
O Lord my God, in thee do I put my trust: save me from all them that persecute me, and deliver me:

Psalm 9:10 (KJV)
And they that know thy name will put their trust in thee: for thou, Lord, hast not forsaken them that seek thee.

Psalm 18:2 (KJV)
The Lord is my rock, and my fortress, and my deliverer; my God, my strength, in whom I will trust; my buckler, and the horn of my salvation, and my high tower.

Psalm 18:30 (KJV)
As for God, his way is perfect: the word of the Lord is tried: he is a buckler to all those that trust in him.

Psalm 28:7 (KJV)
The Lord is my strength and my shield; my heart trusted in him, and I am helped: therefore my heart greatly rejoiceth; and with my song will I praise him.

Psalm 34:8 (KJV)
O taste and see that the Lord is good: blessed is the man that trusteth in him.

Psalm 37:5 (KJV)
Commit thy way unto the Lord; trust also in him; and he shall bring it to pass.

Focus on the Promise and not the Problem

Walking in Faith/Confidence –

Psalm 36:5 (KJV)
Thy mercy, O Lord, is in the heavens; and thy faithfulness reacheth unto the clouds.

Psalm 46:10 (KJV)
Be still, and know that I am God: I will be exalted among the heathen, I will be exalted in the earth.

Psalm 89:1 K (KJV)
I will sing of the mercies of the Lord for ever: with my mouth will I make known thy faithfulness to all generations.

Psalm 89:2 (KJV)
For I have said, Mercy shall be built up for ever: thy faithfulness shalt thou establish in the very heavens.

Proverbs 3:26 (KJV)
For the Lord shall be thy confidence, and shall keep thy foot from being taken.

Proverbs 28:20 (KJV)
A faithful man shall abound with blessings: but he that maketh haste to be rich shall not be innocent.

John 1:12 (KJV)
But as many as received him, to them gave he power to become the sons of God, even to them that believe on his name:

John 3:16 (KJV)
For God so loved the world, that he gave his only begotten Son, that whosoever believeth in him should not perish, but have everlasting life.

Focus on the Promise and not the Problem

Walking in Faith/Confidence –

Galatians 5:22 (KJV)
But the fruit of the Spirit is love, joy, peace, longsuffering, gentleness, goodness, faith,

Ephesians 3:12 (KJV)
In whom we have boldness and access with confidence by the faith of him.

Hebrews 4:16 (KJV)
Let us therefore come boldly unto the throne of grace, that we may obtain mercy, and find grace to help in time of need.

Hebrews 11:1 (KJV)
Now faith is the substance of things hoped for, the evidence of things not seen.

Hebrews 13:5 (KJV)
Let your conversation be without covetousness; and be content with such things as ye have: for he hath said, I will never leave thee, nor forsake thee.

Hebrews 13:8 (KJV)
Jesus Christ the same yesterday, and today, and forever.

Jeremiah 17:7 (KJV)
Blessed is the man that trusteth in the Lord, and whose hope the Lord is.

Psalm 27:13 (KJV)
I had fainted, unless I had believed to see the goodness of the Lord in the land of the living.

Focus on the Promise and not the Problem

Walking in Patience –

Psalm 37:7 (KJV)
Rest in the Lord, and wait patiently for him: fret not thyself because of him who prospereth in his way, because of the man who bringeth wicked devices to pass.

Psalm 40:1-3 (KJV)
I waited patiently for the Lord; and he inclined unto me, and heard my cry. He brought me up also out of an horrible pit, out of the miry clay, and set my feet upon a rock, and established my goings. And he hath put a new song in my mouth, even praise unto our God: many shall see it, and fear, and shall trust in the Lord.

Ecclesiastes 7:8 (KJV)
Better is the end of a thing than the beginning thereof: and the patient in spirit is better than the proud in spirit.

Luke 8:15 (KJV)
But that on the good ground are they, which in an honest and good heart, having heard the word, keep it, and bring forth fruit with patience.

Hebrews 12:1-2 (KJV)
Wherefore seeing we also are compassed about with so great a cloud of witnesses, let us lay aside every weight, and the sin which doth so easily beset us, and let us run with patience the race that is set before us, Looking unto Jesus the author and finisher of our faith; who for the joy that was set before him endured the cross, despising the shame, and is set down at the right hand of the throne of God.

Focus on the Promise and not the Problem

Walking in Patience –

James 1:4 (KJV)
But let patience have her perfect work, that ye may be perfect and entire, wanting nothing.

James 5:7-8 (KJV)
Be patient therefore, brethren, unto the coming of the Lord. Behold, the husbandman waiteth for the precious fruit of the earth, and hath long patience for it, until he receive the early and latter rain. Be ye also patient; stablish your hearts: for the coming of the Lord draweth nigh.

2 Peter 1:6 (KJV)
And to knowledge temperance; and to temperance patience; and to patience godliness;

Colossians 1:9-12 (KJV)
For this cause we also, since the day we heard it, do not cease to pray for you, and to desire that ye might be filled with the knowledge of his will in all wisdom and spiritual understanding; That ye might walk worthy of the Lord unto all pleasing, being fruitful in every good work, and increasing in the knowledge of God; Strengthened with all might, according to his glorious power, unto all patience and longsuffering with joyfulness; Giving thanks unto the Father, which hath made us meet to be partakers of the inheritance of the saints in light:

Focus on the Promise and not the Problem

Walking in Hope –

Psalm 16:9 (KJV)
Therefore my heart is glad, and my glory rejoiceth: my flesh also shall rest in hope.

Psalm 31:24 (KJV)
Be of good courage, and he shall strengthen your heart, all ye that hope in the Lord.

Psalm 33:18 (KJV)
Behold, the eye of the Lord is upon them that fear him, upon them that hope in his mercy;

Psalm 42:5 (KJV)
Why art thou cast down, O my soul? and why art thou disquieted in me? hope thou in God: for I shall yet praise him for the help of his countenance.

Psalm 147:11 (KJV)
The Lord taketh pleasure in them that fear him, in those that hope in his mercy.

Lamentations 3:24 (KJV)
The Lord is my portion, saith my soul; therefore will I hope in him.

Romans 12:12 (KJV)
Rejoicing in hope; patient in tribulation; continuing instant in prayer;

Focus on the Promise and not the Problem

Walking in Hope –

Romans 15:13 (KJV)
Now the God of hope fill you with all joy and peace in believing, that ye may abound in hope, through the power of the Holy Ghost.

1 Timothy 1:1 (KJV)
Paul, an apostle of Jesus Christ by the commandment of God our Saviour, and Lord Jesus Christ, which is our hope;

Hebrews 6:11 (KJV)
And we desire that every one of you do shew the same diligence to the full assurance of hope unto the end:

1 Peter 1:21 (KJV)
Who by him do believe in God, that raised him up from the dead, and gave him glory; that your faith and hope might be in God.

1 John 3:2-3 (KJV)
Beloved, now are we the sons of God, and it doth not yet appear what we shall be: but we know that, when he shall appear, we shall be like him; for we shall see him as he is. And every man that hath this hope in him purifieth himself, even as he is pure.

Isaiah 40:31 (KJV)
But they that wait upon the Lord shall renew their strength; they shall mount up with wings as eagles; they shall run, and not be weary; and they shall walk, and not faint.

Focus on the Promise and not the Problem

Walking in Peace –

Psalm 34:14 (KJV)
Depart from evil, and do good; seek peace, and pursue it.

Proverbs 15:1 (KJV)
A soft answer turneth away wrath: but grievous words stir up anger.

Isaiah 9:6 (KJV)
For unto us a child is born, unto us a son is given: and the government shall be upon his shoulder: and his name shall be called Wonderful, Counsellor, The mighty God, The everlasting Father, The Prince of Peace.

Isaiah 26:3-4 (KJV)
Thou wilt keep him in perfect peace, whose mind is stayed on thee: because he trusteth in thee. Trust ye in the Lord for ever: for in the Lord Jehovah is everlasting strength:

Romans 14:17 (KJV)
For the kingdom of God is not meat and drink; but righteousness, and peace, and joy in the Holy Ghost.

Romans 12:18 (KJV)
If it be possible, as much as lieth in you, live peaceably with all men

Philippians 4:7 (KJV)
And the peace of God, which passeth all understanding, shall keep your hearts and minds through Christ Jesus.

Focus on the Promise and not the Problem

Walking in Peace –

Colossians 3:15 (KJV)
And let the peace of God rule in your hearts, to the which also ye are called in one body; and be ye thankful.

Hebrews 12:14 (KJV)
Follow peace with all men, and holiness, without which no man shall see the Lord:

James 3:18 (KJV)
And the fruit of righteousness is sown in peace of them that make peace.

John 14:27 (KJV)
Peace I leave with you, my peace I give unto you: not as the world giveth, give I unto you. Let not your heart be troubled, neither let it be afraid.

Romans 5:1 (KJV)
Therefore being justified by faith, we have peace with God through our Lord Jesus Christ:

Romans 8:6 (KJV)
For to be carnally minded is death; but to be spiritually minded is life and peace.

Romans 14:17 (KJV)
For the kingdom of God is not meat and drink; but righteousness, and peace, and joy in the Holy Ghost.

2 Corinthians 13:11 (KJV)
Finally, brethren, farewell. Be perfect, be of good comfort, be of one mind, live in peace; and the God of love and peace shall be with you.

When the Son Speaks a Promise for the Needs of Others

Deliverance from Satan and His Demonic Forces –

Ephesians 6:13 (KJV)
Wherefore take unto you the whole armour of God, that ye may be able to withstand in the evil day, and having done all, to stand.

Ephesians 6:17 (KJV)
And take the helmet of salvation, and the sword of the Spirit, which is the word of God:

Luke 10:19 (KJV)
Behold, I give unto you power to tread on serpents and scorpions, and over all the power of the enemy: and nothing shall by any means hurt you.

James 4:7 (KJV)
Submit yourselves therefore to God. Resist the devil, and he will flee from you.

1 Samuel 17:47 (KJV)
And all this assembly shall know that the Lord saveth not with sword and spear: for the battle is the Lord's, and he will give you into our hands.

Deliverance from Satan and His Demonic Forces –

2 Corinthians 10:4 (KJV)
For the weapons of our warfare are not carnal, but mighty through God to the pulling down of strong holds;

2 Chronicles 20:15 (KJV)
And he said, Hearken ye, all Judah, and ye inhabitants of Jerusalem, and thou king Jehoshaphat, Thus saith the Lord unto you, Be not afraid nor dismayed by reason of this great multitude; for the battle is not yours, but God's.

Psalm 94:22 (KJV)
But the Lord is my defense; and my God is the rock of my refuge.

Isaiah 58:6 (KJV)
Is not this the fast that I have chosen? to loose the bands of wickedness, to undo the heavy burdens, and to let the oppressed go free, and that ye break every yoke?

Matthew 18:18 (KJV)
Verily I say unto you, Whatsoever ye shall bind on earth shall be bound in heaven: and whatsoever ye shall loose on earth shall be loosed in heaven.

Isaiah 59:19 (KJV)
So shall they fear the name of the Lord from the west, and his glory from the rising of the sun. When the enemy shall come in like a flood, the Spirit of the Lord shall lift up a standard against him.

Focus on the Promise and not the Problem

Employment –

Isaiah 55:11 (KJV)
So shall my word be that goeth forth out of my mouth: it shall not return unto me void, but it shall accomplish that which I please, and it shall prosper in the thing whereto I sent it.

Isaiah 41:10 (KJV)
Fear thou not; for I am with thee: be not dismayed; for I am thy God: I will strengthen thee; yea, I will help thee; yea, I will uphold thee with the right hand of my righteousness.

Revelation 3:8 (KJV)
I know thy works: behold, I have set before thee an open door, and no man can shut it: for thou hast a little strength, and hast kept my word, and hast not denied my name.

John 16:33 (KJV)
These things I have spoken unto you, that in me ye might have peace. In the world ye shall have tribulation: but be of good cheer; I have overcome the world.

Philippians 4:6-7 (KJV)
Be careful for nothing; but in everything by prayer and supplication with thanksgiving let your requests be made known unto God. And the peace of God, which passeth all understanding, shall keep your hearts and minds through Christ Jesus.

James 1:2-4 (KJV)
My brethren, count it all joy when ye fall into divers temptations; Knowing this, that the trying of your faith worketh patience. But let patience have her perfect work, that ye may be perfect and entire, wanting nothing.

Peace in a Troubled Marriage –

Genesis 2:24 (KJV)
Therefore shall a man leave his father and his mother, and shall cleave unto his wife: and they shall be one flesh.

Ephesians 5:21 (KJV)
Submitting yourselves one to another in the fear of God.

Ephesians 4:31-32 (KJV)
Let all bitterness, and wrath, and anger, and clamour, and evil speaking, be put away from you, with all malice: And be ye kind one to another, tenderhearted, forgiving one another, even as God for Christ's sake hath forgiven you.

Ephesians 4:23-24 (KJV)
And be renewed in the spirit of your mind; And that ye put on the new man, which after God is created in righteousness and true holiness.

1 Peter 3:8-10 (KJV)
Finally, be ye all of one mind, having compassion one of another, love as brethren, be pitiful, be courteous: Not rendering evil for evil, or railing for railing: but contrariwise blessing; knowing that ye are thereunto called, that ye should inherit a blessing. For he that will love life, and see good days, let him refrain his tongue from evil, and his lips that they speak no guile:

Proverbs 3:5-6 (KJV)
Trust in the Lord with all thine heart; and lean not unto thine own understanding. In all thy ways acknowledge him, and he shall direct thy paths.

Focus on the Promise and not the Problem

Overcoming Rejection in Marriage –

Galatians 1:4 (KJV)
Who gave himself for our sins, that he might deliver us from this present evil world, according to the will of God and our Father:

John 8:36 (KJV)
If the Son therefore shall make you free, ye shall be free indeed.

Ephesians 1:16 (KJV)
Cease not to give thanks for you, making mention of you in my prayers;

Luke 4:18 (KJV)
The Spirit of the Lord is upon me, because he hath anointed me to preach the gospel to the poor; he hath sent me to heal the brokenhearted, to preach deliverance to the captives, and recovering of sight to the blind, to set at liberty them that are bruised,

Colossians 3:12-14 (KJV)
Put on therefore, as the elect of God, holy and beloved, bowels of mercies, kindness, humbleness of mind, meekness, longsuffering; Forbearing one another, and forgiving one another, if any man have a quarrel against any: even as Christ forgave you, so also do ye.

And above all these things put on charity, which is the bond of perfectness.

1 Corinthians 13:11 (KJV)
When I was a child, I spake as a child, I understood as a child, I thought as a child: but when I became a man, I put away childish things.

Focus on the Promise and not the Problem

Husbands/Wives –

Ephesians 5:25-26 (KJV)
Husbands, love your wives, even as Christ also loved the church, and gave himself for it; That he might sanctify and cleanse it with the washing of water by the word,

Ephesians 5:22-23 (KJV)
Wives, submit yourselves unto your own husbands, as unto the Lord. For the husband is the head of the wife, even as Christ is the head of the church: and he is the saviour of the body.

1 Corinthians 7:3-5 (KJV)
Let the husband render unto the wife due benevolence: and likewise also the wife unto the husband. The wife hath not power of her own body, but the husband: and likewise also the husband hath not power of his own body, but the wife. Defraud ye not one the other, except it be with consent for a time, that ye may give yourselves to fasting and prayer; and come together again, that Satan tempt you not for your incontinency.

Proverbs 18:22 (KJV)
Whoso findeth a wife findeth a good thing, and obtaineth favour of the Lord.

1 Peter 3:7-8 (KJV)
Likewise, ye husbands, dwell with them according to knowledge, giving honour unto the wife, as unto the weaker vessel, and as being heirs together of the grace of life; that your prayers be not hindered. Finally, be ye all of one mind, having compassion one of another, love as brethren, be pitiful, be courteous:

Focus on the Promise and not the Problem

Child's Future –

Psalm 127:3 (KJV)
Lo, children are a heritage of the Lord: and the fruit of the womb is his reward.

Isaiah 54:13 (KJV)
And all thy children shall be taught of the Lord; and great shall be the peace of thy children.

Proverbs 22:6 (KJV)
Train up a child in the way he should go: and when he is old, he will not depart from it.

Ephesians 6:4 (KJV)
And, ye fathers, provoke not your children to wrath: but bring them up in the nurture and admonition of the Lord.

Deuteronomy 6:7 (KJV)
And thou shalt teach them diligently unto thy children, and shalt talk of them when thou sittest in thine house, and when thou walkest by the way, and when thou liest down, and when thou risest up.

Luke 2:52 (KJV)
And Jesus increased in wisdom and stature, and in favour with God and man.

1 Thessalonians 5:22-25 (KJV)
Abstain from all appearance of evil. And the very God of peace sanctify you wholly; and I pray God your whole spirit and soul and body be preserved blameless unto the coming of our Lord Jesus Christ. Faithful is he that calleth you, who also will do it. Brethren, pray for us.

Focus on the Promise and not the Problem

Rebellious Teenager –

Malachi 4:6 (KJV)
And he shall turn the heart of the fathers to the children, and the heart of the children to their fathers, lest I come and smite the earth with a curse.

Luke 1:16-17 (KJV)
And many of the children of Israel shall he turn to the Lord their God. And he shall go before him in the spirit and power of Elias, to turn the hearts of the fathers to the children, and the disobedient to the wisdom of the just; to make ready a people prepared for the Lord.

Ecclesiastes 12:1 (KJV)
Remember now thy Creator in the days of thy youth, while the evil days come not, nor the years draw nigh, when thou shalt say, I have no pleasure in them.

Proverbs 8:6-7 (KJV)
Hear; for I will speak of excellent things; and the opening of my lips shall be right things. For my mouth shall speak truth; and wickedness is an abomination to my lips.

Proverbs 22:6 (KJV)
Train up a child in the way he should go: and when he is old, he will not depart from it.

Proverbs 13:1 (KJV)
A wise son heareth his father's instruction: but a scorner heareth not rebuke.

Focus on the Promise and not the Problem

Rebellious Teenager –

Ephesians 6:1-3 (KJV)
Children, obey your parents in the Lord: for this is right. Honour thy father and mother; which is the first commandment with promise; That it may be well with thee, and thou mayest live long on the earth.

Isaiah 54:13 (KJV)
And all thy children shall be taught of the Lord; and great shall be the peace of thy children.

Colossians 3:21 (KJV)
Fathers, provoke not your children to anger, lest they be discouraged.

Isaiah 61:1 (KJV)
The Spirit of the Lord God is upon me; because the Lord hath anointed me to preach good tidings unto the meek; he hath sent me to bind up the brokenhearted, to proclaim liberty to the captives, and the opening of the prison to them that are bound;

John 16:13 (KJV)
Howbeit when he, the Spirit of truth, is come, he will guide you into all truth: for he shall not speak of himself; but whatsoever he shall hear, that shall he speak: and he will shew you things to come.

John 20:23 (KJV)
Whosoever sins ye remit, they are remitted unto them; and whosoever sins ye retain, they are retained

When the Son Speaks a Promise Concerning Personal Concerns

Living Free from Worry –

Psalm 34:1 (KJV)
Depart from evil, and do good; seek peace, and pursue it.

Psalm 55:22 (KJV)
Cast thy burden upon the Lord, and he shall sustain thee: he shall never suffer the righteous to be moved.

Psalm 138:8 (KJV)
The Lord will perfect that which concerneth me: thy mercy, O Lord, endureth for ever: forsake not the works of thine own hands.

Proverbs 16:7 (KJV)
When a man's ways please the Lord, he maketh even his enemies to be at peace with him.

Isaiah 26:3 (KJV)
Thou wilt keep him in perfect peace, whose mind is stayed on thee: because he trusteth in thee.

John 14:27 (KJV)
Peace I leave with you, my peace I give unto you: not as the world giveth, give I unto you. Let not your heart be troubled, neither let it be afraid.

Focus on the Promise and not the Problem

Living Free from Worry –

Romans 8:38-39 (KJV)
For I am persuaded, that neither death, nor life, nor angels, nor principalities, nor powers, nor things present, nor things to come, Nor height, nor depth, nor any other creature, shall be able to separate us from the love of God, which is in Christ Jesus our Lord.

Colossians 3:15 (KJV)
And let the peace of God rule in your hearts, to the which also ye are called in one body; and be ye thankful.

2 Corinthians 10:5 (KJV)
Casting down imaginations, and every high thing that exalteth itself against the knowledge of God, and bringing into captivity every thought to the obedience of Christ

Philippians 4:8 (KJV)
Finally, brethren, whatsoever things are true, whatsoever things are honest, whatsoever things are just, whatsoever things are pure, whatsoever things are lovely, whatsoever things are of good report; if there be any virtue, and if there be any praise, think on these things.

1 Peter 5:7 (KJV)
Casting all your care upon him; for he careth for you.

1 John 4:18 (KJV)
There is no fear in love; but perfect love casteth out fear: because fear hath torment. He that feareth is not made perfect in love.

Victory Over Fear –

Exodus 14:13 (KJV)
And Moses said unto the people, Fear ye not, stand still, and see the salvation of the Lord, which he will shew to you today: for the Egyptians whom ye have seen today, ye shall see them again no more for ever.

Psalm 23:4 (KJV)
Yea, though I walk through the valley of the shadow of death, I will fear no evil: for thou art with me; thy rod and thy staff they comfort me.

Psalm 27:1 (KJV)
The Lord is my light and my salvation; whom shall I fear? the Lord is the strength of my life; of whom shall I be afraid?

Psalm 34:4 (KJV)
I sought the Lord, and he heard me, and delivered me from all my fears.

Psalm 46:1 (KJV)
God is our refuge and strength, a very present help in trouble.

Psalm 56:3-4 (KJV)
What time I am afraid, I will trust in thee. In God I will praise his word, in God I have put my trust; I will not fear what flesh can do unto me.

Focus on the Promise and not the Problem

Victory Over Fear –

Proverbs 3:25-26 (KJV)
Be not afraid of sudden fear, neither of the desolation of the wicked, when it cometh. For the Lord shall be thy confidence, and shall keep thy foot from being taken.

Isaiah 54:14 (KJV)
In righteousness shalt thou be established: thou shalt be far from oppression; for thou shalt not fear: and from terror; for it shall not come near thee.

John 14:27 (KJV)
Peace I leave with you, my peace I give unto you: not as the world giveth, give I unto you. Let not your heart be troubled, neither let it be afraid.

Romans 8:15 (KJV)
For ye have not received the spirit of bondage again to fear; but ye have received the Spirit of adoption, whereby we cry, Abba, Father.

2 Timothy 1:7 (KJV)
For God hath not given us the spirit of fear; but of power, and of love, and of a sound mind.

Hebrews 13:6 (KJV)
So that we may boldly say, The Lord is my helper, and I will not fear what man shall do unto me.

1 John 4:18 (KJV)
There is no fear in love; but perfect love casteth out fear: because fear hath torment. He that feareth is not made perfect in love.

Focus on the Promise and not the Problem

Renewing Your Mind –

Joshua 1:8 (KJV)
This book of the law shall not depart out of thy mouth; but thou shalt meditate therein day and night, that thou mayest observe to do according to all that is written therein: for then thou shalt make thy way prosperous, and then thou shalt have good success.

Proverbs 16:3 (KJV)
Commit thy works unto the Lord, and thy thoughts shall be established.

Isaiah 26:3 (KJV)
Thou wilt keep him in perfect peace, whose mind is stayed on thee: because he trusteth in thee.

Romans 12:2 (KJV)
And be not conformed to this world: but be ye transformed by the renewing of your mind, that ye may prove what is that good, and acceptable, and perfect, will of God.

2 Corinthians 10:5 (KJV)
Casting down imaginations, and every high thing that exalteth itself against the knowledge of God, and bringing into captivity every thought to the obedience of Christ;

Ephesians 4:23 (KJV)
And be renewed in the spirit of your mind;

Philippians 2:5 (KJV)
Let this mind be in you, which was also in Christ Jesus:

When Trouble Hit Your Life –

Psalm 9:9 (KJV)
The Lord also will be a refuge for the oppressed, a refuge in times of trouble.

Psalm 27:5-6 (KJV)
For in the time of trouble he shall hide me in his pavilion: in the secret of his tabernacle shall he hide me; he shall set me up upon a rock. And now shall mine head be lifted up above mine enemies round about me: therefore will I offer in his tabernacle sacrifices of joy; I will sing, yea, I will sing praises unto the Lord.

Psalm 34:17-19 (KJV)
The righteous cry, and the Lord heareth, and delivereth them out of all their troubles. The Lord is nigh unto them that are of a broken heart; and saveth such as be of a contrite spirit. Many are the afflictions of the righteous: but the Lord delivereth him out of them all.

Psalm 46:1 (KJV)
God is our refuge and strength, a very present help in trouble.

Psalm 57:1 (KJV)
Be merciful unto me, O God, be merciful unto me: for my soul trusteth in thee: yea, in the shadow of thy wings will I make my refuge, until these calamities be overpast.

John 14:27 (KJV)
Peace I leave with you, my peace I give unto you: not as the world giveth, give I unto you. Let not your heart be troubled, neither let it be afraid.

Focus on the Promise and not the Problem

Living Free from Depression –

Psalm 3:4 (KJV)
I cried unto the Lord with my voice, and he heard me out of his holy hill. Selah.

Psalm 40:2 (KJV)
He brought me up also out of an horrible pit, out of the miry clay, and set my feet upon a rock, and established my goings.

Psalm 43:2-4 (KJV)
For thou art the God of my strength: why dost thou cast me off? why go I mourning because of the oppression of the enemy? O send out thy light and thy truth: let them lead me; let them bring me unto thy holy hill, and to thy tabernacles. Then will I go unto the altar of God, unto God my exceeding joy: yea, upon the harp will I praise thee, O God my God.

Psalm 116:8-9 (KJV)
For thou hast delivered my soul from death, mine eyes from tears, and my feet from falling. I will walk before the Lord in the land of the living.

Proverbs 3:5-6 (KJV)
Trust in the Lord with all thine heart; and lean not unto thine own understanding. In all thy ways acknowledge him, and he shall direct thy paths.

Isaiah 26:3 (KJV)
Thou wilt keep him in perfect peace, whose mind is stayed on thee: because he trusteth in thee.

Living Free from Depression –

Isaiah 35:4 (KJV)
Say to them that are of a fearful heart, Be strong, fear not: behold, your God will come with vengeance, even God with a recompence; he will come and save you.

Isaiah 61:3 (KJV)
To appoint unto them that mourn in Zion, to give unto them beauty for ashes, the oil of joy for mourning, the garment of praise for the spirit of heaviness; that they might be called trees of righteousness, the planting of the Lord, that he might be glorified.

Jeremiah 29:11 (KJV)
For I know the thoughts that I think toward you, saith the Lord, thoughts of peace, and not of evil, to give you an expected end.

Luke 4:18 (KJV)
The Spirit of the Lord is upon me, because he hath anointed me to preach the gospel to the poor; he hath sent me to heal the brokenhearted, to preach deliverance to the captives, and recovering of sight to the blind, to set at liberty them that are bruised,

John 14:27 (KJV)
Peace I leave with you, my peace I give unto you: not as the world giveth, give I unto you. Let not your heart be troubled, neither let it be afraid.

Focus on the Promise and not the Problem

Walking in Freedom –

Isaiah 61:1-3 (KJV)
The Spirit of the Lord God is upon me; because the Lord hath anointed me to preach good tidings unto the meek; he hath sent me to bind up the brokenhearted, to proclaim liberty to the captives, and the opening of the prison to them that are bound; To proclaim the acceptable year of the Lord, and the day of vengeance of our God; to comfort all that mourn; To appoint unto them that mourn in Zion, to give unto them beauty for ashes, the oil of joy for mourning, the garment of praise for the spirit of heaviness; that they might be called trees of righteousness, the planting of the Lord, that he might be glorified.

Luke 4:18 (KJV)
The Spirit of the Lord is upon me, because he hath anointed me to preach the gospel to the poor; he hath sent me to heal the brokenhearted, to preach deliverance to the captives, and recovering of sight to the blind, to set at liberty them that are bruised,

Matthew 10:8 (KJV)
Heal the sick, cleanse the lepers, raise the dead, cast out devils: freely ye have received, freely give.

Romans 8:21 (KJV)
Because the creature itself also shall be delivered from the bondage of corruption into the glorious liberty of the children of God.

Walking in Freedom –

2 Corinthians 3:17-18 (KJV)
Now the Lord is that Spirit: and where the Spirit of the Lord is, there is liberty. But we all, with open face beholding as in a glass the glory of the Lord, are changed into the same image from glory to glory, even as by the Spirit of the Lord.

Galatians 5:1 (KJV)
Stand fast therefore in the liberty wherewith Christ hath made us free, and be not entangled again with the yoke of bondage.

Galatians 5:13 (KJV)
For, brethren, ye have been called unto liberty; only use not liberty for an occasion to the flesh, but by love serve one another.

John 8:36 (KJV)
If the Son therefore shall make you free, ye shall be free indeed.

Living Free from Guilt –

Psalm 119:9-11 (KJV)
Wherewithal shall a young man cleanse his way? by taking heed thereto according to thy word. With my whole heart have I sought thee: O let me not wander from thy commandments. Thy word have I hid in mine heart, that I might not sin against thee.

Psalm 103:8-12 (KJV)
The Lord is merciful and gracious, slow to anger, and plenteous in mercy. He will not always chide: neither will he keep his anger for ever. He hath not dealt with us after our sins; nor rewarded us according to our iniquities. For as the heaven is high above the earth, so great is his mercy toward them that fear him. As far as the east is from the west, so far hath he removed our transgressions from us.

2 Corinthians 5:21 (KJV)
For he hath made him to be sin for us, who knew no sin; that we might be made the righteousness of God in him.

Ephesians 4:30-32 (KJV)
And grieve not the holy Spirit of God, whereby ye are sealed unto the day of redemption. Let all bitterness, and wrath, and anger, and clamour, and evil speaking, be put away from you, with all malice: And be ye kind one to another, tenderhearted, forgiving one another, even as God for Christ's sake hath forgiven you.

Hebrews 8:12 (KJV)
For I will be merciful to their unrighteousness, and their sins and their iniquities will I remember no more.

Focus on the Promise and not the Problem

Living Free from Loneliness –

Proverbs 18:24 (KJV)
A man that hath friends must shew himself friendly: and there is a friend that sticketh closer than a brother.

John 14:16-18 (KJV)
And I will pray the Father, and he shall give you another Comforter, that he may abide with you for ever; Even the Spirit of truth; whom the world cannot receive, because it seeth him not, neither knoweth him: but ye know him; for he dwelleth with you, and shall be in you. I will not leave you comfortless: I will come to you.

Hebrews 10:25 (KJV)
Not forsaking the assembling of ourselves together, as the manner of some is; but exhorting one another: and so much the more, as ye see the day approaching.

Hebrews 13:5 (KJV)
Let your conversation be without covetousness; and be content with such things as ye have: for he hath said, I will never leave thee, nor forsake thee.

1 John 1:3-4 (KJV)
That which we have seen and heard declare we unto you, that ye also may have fellowship with us: and truly our fellowship is with the Father, and with his Son Jesus Christ. And these things write we unto you, that your joy may be full.

Living Free from a Negative Self-Concept –

Genesis 1:26 (KJV)
And God said, Let us make man in our image, after our likeness: and let them have dominion over the fish of the sea, and over the fowl of the air, and over the cattle, and over all the earth, and over every creeping thing that creepeth upon the earth.

Proverbs 3:6 (KJV)
In all thy ways acknowledge him, and he shall direct thy paths.

Romans 8:1 (KJV)
There is therefore now no condemnation to them which are in Christ Jesus, who walk not after the flesh, but after the Spirit.

Romans 8:38-39 (KJV)
For I am persuaded, that neither death, nor life, nor angels, nor principalities, nor powers, nor things present, nor things to come, Nor height, nor depth, nor any other creature, shall be able to separate us from the love of God, which is in Christ Jesus our Lord.

2 Corinthians 5:17 (KJV)
Therefore if any man be in Christ, he is a new creature: old things are passed away; behold, all things are become new.

2 Corinthians 12:9 (KJV)
And he said unto me, My grace is sufficient for thee: for my strength is made perfect in weakness. Most gladly therefore will I rather glory in my infirmities, that the power of Christ may rest upon me.

Living Free from a Negative Self-Concept –

Ephesians 2:10 (KJV)
For we are his workmanship, created in Christ Jesus unto good works, which God hath before ordained that we should walk in them.

Philippians 1:6 (KJV)
Being confident of this very thing, that he which hath begun a good work in you will perform it until the day of Jesus Christ:

Colossians 2:10 (KJV)
And ye are complete in him, which is the head of all principality and power:

Colossians 3:10 (KJV)
And have put on the new man, which is renewed in knowledge after the image of him that created him:

Colossians 4:12 (KJV)
Epaphras, who is one of you, a servant of Christ, saluteth you, always labouring fervently for you in prayers, that ye may stand perfect and complete in all the will of God.

Deuteronomy 28:13 (KJV)
And the Lord shall make thee the head, and not the tail; and thou shalt be above only, and thou shalt not be beneath; if that thou hearken unto the commandments of the Lord thy God, which I command thee this day, to observe and to do them:

Living Free from Rejection –

Psalm 27:9-11 (KJV)
Hide not thy face far from me; put not thy servant away in anger: thou hast been my help; leave me not, neither forsake me, O God of my salvation. When my father and my mother forsake me, then the Lord will take me up. Teach me thy way, O Lord, and lead me in a plain path, because of mine enemies.

Isaiah 53:3 (KJV)
He is despised and rejected of men; a man of sorrows, and acquainted with grief: and we hid as it were our faces from him; he was despised, and we esteemed him not.

Mark 15:16-20 (KJV)
And the soldiers led him away into the hall, called Praetorium; and they call together the whole band. And they clothed him with purple, and platted a crown of thorns, and put it about his head, And began to salute him, Hail, King of the Jews! And they smote him on the head with a reed, and did spit upon him, and bowing their knees worshipped him. And when they had mocked him, they took off the purple from him, and put his own clothes on him, and led him out to crucify him.

Mark 15:34 (KJV)
And at the ninth hour Jesus cried with a loud voice, saying, Eloi, Eloi, lama sabachthani? which is, being interpreted, My God, my God, why hast thou forsaken me?

Living Free from Rejection –

2 Corinthians 4:7-10 (KJV)
But we have this treasure in earthen vessels, that the excellency of the power may be of God, and not of us. We are troubled on every side, yet not distressed; we are perplexed, but not in despair; Persecuted, but not forsaken; cast down, but not destroyed; Always bearing about in the body the dying of the Lord Jesus, that the life also of Jesus might be made manifest in our body.

2 Corinthians 4:7-10 (KJV)
But we have this treasure in earthen vessels, that the excellency of the power may be of God, and not of us. We are troubled on every side, yet not distressed; we are perplexed, but not in despair; Persecuted, but not forsaken; cast down, but not destroyed; Always bearing about in the body the dying of the Lord Jesus, that the life also of Jesus might be made manifest in our body.

Hebrews 13:5-8 (KJV)
Let your conversation be without covetousness; and be content with such things as ye have: for he hath said, I will never leave thee, nor forsake thee. So that we may boldly say, The Lord is my helper, and I will not fear what man shall do unto me. Remember them which have the rule over you, who have spoken unto you the word of God: whose faith follow, considering the end of their conversation. Jesus Christ the same yesterday, and today, and for\
ever.

Walking in Forgiveness –

Matthew 5:23-24 (KJV)
Therefore if thou bring thy gift to the altar, and there rememberest that thy brother hath ought against thee; Leave there thy gift before the altar, and go thy way; first be reconciled to thy brother, and then come and offer thy gift.

Matthew 18:21-22 (KJV)
Then came Peter to him, and said, Lord, how oft shall my brother sin against me, and I forgive him? till seven times? Jesus saith unto him, I say not unto thee, Until seven times: but, Until seventy times seven.

Mark 11:24-26 (KJV)
Therefore I say unto you, What things soever ye desire, when ye pray, believe that ye receive them, and ye shall have them. And when ye stand praying, forgive, if ye have ought against any: that your Father also which is in heaven may forgive you your trespasses. But if ye do not forgive, neither will your Father which is in heaven forgive your trespasses.

Colossians 3:13 (KJV)
Forbearing one another, and forgiving one another, if any man have a quarrel against any: even as Christ forgave you, so also do ye.

1 John 1:9 (KJV)
If we confess our sins, he is faithful and just to forgive us our sins, and to cleanse us from all unrighteousness.

When the Son Speaks a Promise About Caring for Others

Comforting Others –

Isaiah 40:1 (KJV)
Comfort ye, comfort ye my people, saith your God.

Isaiah 61:3 (KJV)
To appoint unto them that mourn in Zion, to give unto them beauty for ashes, the oil of joy for mourning, the garment of praise for the spirit of heaviness; that they might be called trees of righteousness, the planting of the Lord, that he might be glorified.

Isaiah 66:13 (KJV)
As one whom his mother comforteth, so will I comfort you; and ye shall be comforted in Jerusalem.

Matthew 5:4 (KJV)
Blessed are they that mourn: for they shall be comforted.

John 14:16-18 (KJV)
And I will pray the Father, and he shall give you another Comforter, that he may abide with you for ever; Even the Spirit of truth; whom the world cannot receive, because it seeth him not, neither knoweth him: but ye know him; for he dwelleth with you, and shall be in you. I will not leave you comfortless: I will come to you.

1 Thessalonians 4:18 (KJV)
Wherefore comfort one another with these words.

Encouraging Others –

1 Samuel 30:6 (KJV)
And David was greatly distressed; for the people spake of stoning him, because the soul of all the people was grieved, every man for his sons and for his daughters: but David encouraged himself in the Lord his God.

Proverbs 15:23 (KJV)
A man hath joy by the answer of his mouth: and a word spoken in due season, how good is it!

John 16:33 (KJV)
These things I have spoken unto you, that in me ye might have peace. In the world ye shall have tribulation: but be of good cheer; I have overcome the world.

1 Corinthians 14:3 (KJV)
But he that prophesieth speaketh unto men to edification, and exhortation, and comfort.

2 Corinthians 1:4 (KJV)
Who comforteth us in all our tribulation, that we may be able to comfort them which are in any trouble, by the comfort wherewith we ourselves are comforted of God.

Ephesians 4:29 (KJV)
Let no corrupt communication proceed out of your mouth, but that which is good to the use of edifying, that it may minister grace unto the hearers.

Praying for Safety and Protection –

Psalm 4:8 (KJV)
I will both lay me down in peace, and sleep: for thou, Lord, only makest me dwell in safety.

Psalm 34:7 (KJV)
The angel of the Lord encampeth round about them that fear him, and delivereth them.

Psalm 91:1-2 (KJV)
He that dwelleth in the secret place of the most High shall abide under the shadow of the Almighty. I will say of the Lord, He is my refuge and my fortress: my God; in him will I trust.

Psalm 91:10-11 (KJV)
There shall no evil befall thee, neither shall any plague come nigh thy dwelling. For he shall give his angels charge over thee, to keep thee in all thy ways.

Psalm 112:7 (KJV)
He shall not be afraid of evil tidings: his heart is fixed, trusting in the Lord.

Proverbs 3:24-26 (KJV)
When thou liest down, thou shalt not be afraid: yea, thou shalt lie down, and thy sleep shall be sweet. Be not afraid of sudden fear, neither of the desolation of the wicked, when it cometh. For the Lord shall be thy confidence, and shall keep thy foot from being taken.

Praying for Safety and Protection –

Proverbs 18:10 (KJV)
The name of the Lord is a strong tower: the righteous runneth into it, and is safe.

Proverbs 29:2 (KJV)
The fear of man bringeth a snare: but whoso putteth his trust in the Lord shall be safe.

Isaiah 26:3 (KJV)
Thou wilt keep him in perfect peace, whose mind is stayed on thee: because he trusteth in thee.

Luke 10:19 (KJV)
Behold, I give unto you power to tread on serpents and scorpions, and over all the power of the enemy: and nothing shall by any means hurt you.

2 Timothy 4:18 (KJV)
And the Lord shall deliver me from every evil work, and will preserve me unto his heavenly kingdom: to whom be glory for ever and ever. Amen.

Praying for Someone Who Has Lost a Loved One –

Ecclesiastes 3:4 (KJV)
A time to weep, and a time to laugh; a time to mourn, and a time to dance;

Matthew 5:4 (KJV)
Blessed are they that mourn: for they shall be comforted.

2 Corinthians 1:4 (KJV)
Who comforteth us in all our tribulation, that we may be able to comfort them which are in any trouble, by the comfort wherewith we ourselves are comforted of God.

Philippians 4:7 (KJV)
And the peace of God, which passeth all understanding, shall keep your hearts and minds through Christ Jesus.

1 Thessalonians 4:13-17 (KJV)
But I would not have you to be ignorant, brethren, concerning them which are asleep, that ye sorrow not, even as others which have no hope. For if we believe that Jesus died and rose again, even so them also which sleep in Jesus will God bring with him. For this we say unto you by the word of the Lord, that we which are alive and remain unto the coming of the Lord shall not prevent them which are asleep. For the Lord himself shall descend from heaven with a shout, with the voice of the archangel, and with the trump of God: and the dead in Christ shall rise first: Then we which are alive and remain shall be caught up together with them in the clouds, to meet the Lord in the air: and so shall we ever be with the Lord.

Salvation for a Loved One –

Luke 13:3 (KJV)
I tell you, Nay: but, except ye repent, ye shall all likewise perish.

John 1:12 (KJV)
But as many as received him, to them gave he power to become the sons of God, even to them that believe on his name:

John 3:16 (KJV)
For God so loved the world, that he gave his only begotten Son, that whosoever believeth in him should not perish, but have everlasting life.

Romans 10:13 (KJV)
For whosoever shall call upon the name of the Lord shall be saved.

Romans 3:22-23 (KJV)
Even the righteousness of God which is by faith of Jesus Christ unto all and upon all them that believe: for there is no difference: For all have sinned, and come short of the glory of God;

Ephesians 2:8-9 (KJV)
For by grace are ye saved through faith; and that not of yourselves: it is the gift of God: Not of works, lest any man should boast.

Salvation for a Loved One –

Titus 3:5 (KJV)
Not by works of righteousness which we have done, but according to his mercy he saved us, by the washing of regeneration, and renewing of the Holy Ghost;

James 5:20 (KJV)
Let him know, that he which converteth the sinner from the error of his way shall save a soul from death, and shall hide a multitude of sins.

2 Peter 3:9 King (KJV)
The Lord is not slack concerning his promise, as some men count slackness; but is longsuffering to us-ward, not willing that any should perish, but that all should come to repentance.

Romans 10:9-10 (KJV)
That if thou shalt confess with thy mouth the Lord Jesus, and shalt believe in thine heart that God hath raised him from the dead, thou shalt be saved. For with the heart man believeth unto righteousness; and with the mouth confession is made unto salvation.

When the Son Speaks a Promise about People and Nations

Nations and Continents –

Psalm 2:8 (KJV)
Ask of me, and I shall give thee the heathen for thine inheritance, and the uttermost parts of the earth for thy possession.

Psalm 72:11 (KJV)
Yea, all kings shall fall down before him: all nations shall serve him.

Proverbs 21:1 (KJV)
The king's heart is in the hand of the Lord, as the rivers of water: he turneth it whithersoever he will.

Haggai 2:7 (KJV)
And I will shake all nations, and the desire of all nations shall come: and I will fill this house with glory, saith the LORD of hosts.

Psalms 67:4 (KJV)
O let the nations be glad and sing for joy: for thou shalt judge the people righteously, and govern the nations upon earth. Selah.

Psalms 22:28 (KJV)
For the kingdom is the LORD'S: and he is the governor among the nations.

School Systems –

Psalm 33:12 (KJV)
Blessed is the nation whose God is the Lord; and the people whom he hath chosen for his own inheritance.

Proverbs 2:10-12 (KJV)
When wisdom entereth into thine heart, and knowledge is pleasant unto thy soul; Discretion shall preserve thee, understanding shall keep thee: To deliver thee from the way of the evil man, from the man that speaketh froward things;

Deuteronomy 31:6 (KJV)
Be strong and courageous. Do not fear or be in dread of them, for it is the Lord your God who goes with you. He will not leave you or forsake you.

Philippians 4:6-7 (KJV)
Do not be anxious about anything, but in everything by prayer and supplication with thanksgiving let your requests be made known to God. And the peace of God, which surpasses all understanding, will guard your hearts and your minds in Christ Jesus.

Proverbs 3:5-6 (KJV)
Trust in the Lord with all your heart, and do not lean on your own understanding. In all your ways acknowledge him, and he will make straight your paths.

Members of the Armed Forces –

Isaiah 26:3 (KJV)
You will keep in perfect peace those whose minds are steadfast, because they trust in you.

2 Corinthians 12:10 (KJV)
That is why, for Christ's sake, I delight in weaknesses, in insults, in hardships, in persecutions, in difficulties. For when I am weak, then I am strong.

Joshua 1:9 (KJV)
Have I not commanded you?
Be strong and courageous. Do not be afraid; do not be discouraged, for the Lord your God will be with you wherever you go.

Psalm 27:13 (KJV)
I remain confident of this: I will see the goodness of the Lord in the land of the living.

Psalm 91:1-2 (KJV)
Whoever dwells in the shelter of the Most High will rest in the shadow of the Almighty. I will say of the Lord, "He is my refuge and my fortress, my God, in whom I trust."

Romans 5:2-5 (KJV)
And we boast in the hope of the glory of God. Not only so, but we also glory in our sufferings, because we know that suffering produces perseverance; perseverance, character; and character, hope. And hope does not put us to shame, because God's love has been poured out into our hearts through the Holy Spirit, who has been given to us.

Focus on the Promise and not the Problem

Members of the Armed Forces –

Proverbs 3:5-6 (KJV)
Trust in the Lord with all your heart and lean not on your own understanding; In all your ways submit to him, and he will make your paths straight.

Deuteronomy 31:6 (KJV)
Be strong and courageous. Do not be afraid or terrified because of them, for the Lord your God goes with you; he will never leave you nor forsake you.

Psalm 61:1-3 (KJV)
Hear my cry, O God; listen to my prayer. From the ends of the earth I call to you, I call as my heart grows faint; lead me to the rock that is higher than I. For you have been my refuge, a strong tower against the foe.

Psalm 46:1-3 (KJV)
God is our refuge and strength, an ever-present help in trouble. Therefore we will not fear, though the earth give way and the mountains fall into the heart of the sea, though its waters roar and foam and the mountains quake with their surging

James 1:2-5 (KJV)
Consider it pure joy, my brothers and sisters, whenever you face trials of many kinds, because you know that the testing of your faith produces perseverance. Let perseverance finish its work so that you may be mature and complete, not lacking anything. If any of you lacks wisdom, you should ask God, who gives generously to all without finding fault, and it will be given to you.

Focus on the Promise and not the Problem

Missionaries –

Matthew 28:19-20 (KJV)
Go ye therefore, and teach all nations, baptizing them in the name of the Father, and of the Son, and of the Holy Ghost: Teaching them to observe all things whatsoever I have commanded you: and, lo, I am with you alway, even unto the end of the world. Amen.

Acts 1:8 (KJV)
But ye shall receive power, after that the Holy Ghost is come upon you: and ye shall be witnesses unto me both in Jerusalem, and in all Judaea, and in Samaria, and unto the uttermost part of the earth.

Mark 16:15 (KJV)
And he said unto them, Go ye into all the world, and preach the gospel to every creature.

Romans 10:14 (KJV)
How then shall they call on him in whom they have not believed? and how shall they believe in him of whom they have not heard? and how shall they hear without a preacher?

Psalms 96:3 (KJV)
Declare his glory among the heathen, his wonders among all people.

Peace of Jerusalem –

Joel 3:14 (KJV)
Multitudes, multitudes in the valley of decision: for the day of the Lord is near in the valley of decision.

Isaiah 45:17 (KJV)
But Israel shall be saved in the Lord with an everlasting salvation: ye shall not be ashamed nor confounded world without end.

Matthew 23:37 (KJV)
O Jerusalem, Jerusalem, thou that killest the prophets, and stonest them which are sent unto thee, how often would I have gathered thy children together, even as a hen gathereth her chickens under her wings, and ye would not!

Philippians 4:7 (KJV)
And the peace of God, which passeth all understanding, shall keep your hearts and minds through Christ Jesus.

Exodus 14:14 (KJV)
The Lord shall fight for you, and ye shall hold your peace.

Psalm 122:6-9 (KJV)
Pray for the peace of Jerusalem: they shall prosper that love thee. Peace be within thy walls, and prosperity within thy palaces. For my brethren and companions' sakes, I will now say, Peace be within thee. Because of the house of the Lord our God I will seek thy good.

Made in the USA
Columbia, SC
12 April 2019